# Widening the Field

# Widening the Field

## Continuing Education in Higher Education

*Edited by* COLIN TITMUS

The Society for Research into
Higher Education & NFER-NELSON

Published by SRHE & NFER-NELSON
At the University, Guildford, Surrey GU2 5XH

First published 1985
© The Society for Research into Higher Education

ISBN 1 85059 012 5
Code 8947 02 1

Typeset and Artwork by FD Graphics, Fleet, Hampshire.
Printed and Bound by Billings, Worcester.

# Contents

# 1

# Higher Education in Continuing Education

## Colin Titmus

This collection of papers appears under the sponsorship of the Society for Research into Higher Education. It offers an up to date discussion of issues relating to continuing education as it is practised in institutions of higher education. It does not claim to be comprehensive in its coverage, even of those matters specifically affecting the United Kingdom, which is the community on which it is principally focused. It does try to address itself to those matters which appear to be fundamental: the current practices and policies of higher education institutions; the arguments for and against their providing continuing education; the nature of this provision and to whom it might be offered; the extent to which higher education is adapted to a continuing education role and how its suitability might be improved; the characteristics and needs of adult learners in higher education, the clients for continuing education; the needs and organization of business and commercial sponsors; the costs and economic benefits of continuing education.

Issues of national policy, of rights to continuing education, and of obligations to provide it are also discussed. To set British practices and problems in a wider perspective there is an account of continuing education in higher education in France, in the Federal Republic of Germany and in Sweden. Finally, the reports of the working parties on continuing education set up by the University Grants Committee (UGC) and the National Advisory Body for public sector higher education (NAB) are jointly analysed and subjected to comment.

The authors have all had considerable experience in higher education or industry. More importantly, as their biographies demonstrate (pp.116-8). they have made distinguished contributions to continuing education in these fields, as educators and administrators and by their research and reflection.

## The Need for Continuing Education

The purpose of this volume is not only to offer a factual review of the current situation, but also to draw attention to research and studies which have already been undertaken in the field and, as befits the aims of the

Society for Research into Higher Education, open up new lines of inquiry. In the whole of continuing education these will be many. Its recognition as a distinctive sector of education is very new. It is clear from the chapters of this book that the precise meaning of the term is not universally agreed. Yet its worldwide development since the Second World War is undeniable.

Although reluctantly in many cases, educators, politicians, employers, employees and other citizens have become aware that a once for all initial education for everybody, whether it ends in the teens or the mid-twenties, is inadequate to the demands of modern living, even in those countries where universal childhood schooling exists. There may be disagreement about forms of education, whether the globally predominant pattern of school systems is the right one, but it is now generally believed that, whatever is done in youth, the well-being of individuals and of the societies in which they live requires further, repeated, if not continuous, learning throughout life.

The reasons advanced for this belief are presented in several chapters here. In principle they do not all require that individuals have access in adult life to a systematic, institutionally-based provision of instruction. Much may be learned incidentally from the experiences of everyday life, and much more from self-directed study, in which, research suggests, a high proportion of adults already engage. In practice, however, for some kinds of learning the participant needs help, and here research suggests that many people need the stimulus of easily available teaching and learning facilities to draw them on to further study. Provision of opportunities creates demand, so evidence indicates. It therefore appears that the amount of study in adult life would be significantly reduced if institutions providing opportunities for it did not exist.

# Involvement of Higher Education

This, of course, is an argument for adult education institutions, it does not in itself call for those in higher education to engage in continuing education. In many countries, over many years, not only university staff but also adult educators believed that universities, the dominant if not the exclusive higher education institutions, were by their nature inappropriate to undertake the education of adults. This was to a large extent due to a limited concept of the nature and target population of adult education, which prevailed until quite recently (if a concept of adult education as a distinctive sector and process of education existed at all) and is still widespread, particularly in the United Kingdom and in countries influenced by the British tradition of education. Indeed, one of the reasons why the term continuing education is increasingly replacing that of adult education is the historical exclusiveness of the latter, which still leads many people to associate it with non-vocational study of a liberal or recreational nature, not sanctioned by any diploma or certificate and intended primarily for the working class. The use of the expression continuing education throughout this book should make it clear that the field to be covered is much wider than that of traditional adult education, although it includes it.

British universities have been engaged in liberal education for over a century and were largely responsible for establishing the concept. It has not prevented them from engaging, in a piecemeal and empirical fashion, in other forms of continuing education, but it may have hindered the formulation of a coherent policy in the field. The public sector of higher education is less traditionally bound and is more oriented towards education for capability but, perhaps in part because of academic drift towards imitation of universities, it is not, according to the NAB report, adequately providing for continuing education. Both the university and the public sector, like the higher education systems of other countries, are under pressure, from inside themselves and from outside, to become major continuing education providers. The arguments for this are many, but they boil down to three: the principle that equality of educational opportunity requires it; the position of higher education institutions as the developers and repositories of knowledge that society needs; the self-interest of the institutions.

## The Consequences of Involvement

This last, the self-interest of the institutions, has been the main trigger for the serious involvement of higher education in continuing education. The slowness and hesitancy which certainly exists in translating concern into wholehearted practice, appears to derive from uncertainty about where that self-interest lies. The considerations are complex. On the one hand the question of its role in continuing education is part of a general debate about the function and governance of higher education. The debate is going on in other European countries, but since it is to a major degree about power and that, not only actually but legally, lies in other countries with the State, it tends to be simpler there. On the other hand, by participating in its provision higher education becomes involved in a wider debate about the nature, purpose and necessity, not only of continuing education, but of other related concepts such as recurrent education and lifelong learning.

Continuing education constitutes an additional element in current arguments about the purposes of the higher education system; about the balance between research and teaching; the persons for whom teaching should be provided; about the kind and level of education to be offered; how institutions should be structured. It is of significance for any decisions about policy, organization and curriculum – and about who should participate in them.

To offer some examples: if it had already become difficult for higher education institutions to maintain that they alone should decide how they should be run, what they should do and to what end, according to their own criteria and without reference to the outside world, it would be even harder if they were providing continuing education. But they cannot avoid the issue even if they do not provide continuing education, because appreciation by external interests of their potential value as agencies of it increases the pressure upon them to do what society, or powerful groups within it, want. Higher education has not responded very enthusiastically to demands that it pay more attention to the teaching and learning needs of its conventional undergraduates. If it takes on continuing education students, who, it seems, have their own learning needs and require different teaching, and perhaps rather more, pressure to take these matters more seriously is likely to increase. In questions of resource allocation continuing education will weigh heavily. It is touted as a source of income and, if it is, that may be an argument for shifting the balance from degree teaching for late teenagers to provision for older people with other needs, on the grounds that traditional activities may benefit from the extra funds.

To these issues the theory and practice of continuing education in general, the study of it and debates about it are relevant, just as these considerations and their resolution are of concern to those engaged in other forms of continuing education. It is true to say that as the nature and purpose of continuing education as generally understood affect the attitude of those in higher education to their participation in it, so conversely the engagement of higher education in it will influence general understanding of its nature, purpose and conditions of operation.

For example, if one takes the issue of the right of adults to education, it is one thing to say that they have that right, it is quite another to say that the right includes higher education. A new element is introduced into the controversy about who should decide what and how much study adults should have a right to. Further it affects the question, if there is a right, whether there is an obligation to provide study opportunities and make them accessible by such offers as paid educational leave. Whose obligation is it and, in particular, whose is the responsibility to pay for it – the State, employers, individual learners? What are the benefits of continuing education and who enjoys them? Should they be judged by purely economic criteria? What other criteria are there and how may assessment be carried out?

## The Need for Research and Study

It cannot be said that a definitive solution has been found to any of the problems raised. The element of value judgement in most of them probably makes it impossible to arrive at a universally acceptable solution. Nevertheless, within any framework of values, crucial choices remain to be made. In order to be true to itself higher education's choices should be informed by empirical research and critical reflection upon experience. In the world of continuing education as a whole a certain amount of both has been undertaken and has proved of value in practice. Less attention has so far been devoted to applying the results to continuing education in higher education, or to studying that area's specific problems. It is significant how much the present authors have drawn on evidence from continuing education outside higher education rather than within it. They reflect the current state of knowledge in Britain. From around 1970 and starting from a lower base, France and Germany appear to have grappled better with the problem.

## What do Commerce and Industry want?

The fault is by no means entirely that of higher education. If society requires universities and public sector institutions to undertake continuing education, then society must formulate what it needs of this activity and make some effort to transmit those needs in a form which institutions can understand and to which they can respond. There should be mutual adaptation between providers and clientele. If higher education has far to go in this, in the view of many, even among their own ranks, the collective clients have further.

Given the market in which continuing education in higher education is called upon to operate, this volume should include some contribution from the employers' side to the sytematic study of what their needs are, how they are identified and how they are to be met. It is not there. According to research, the most frequent motivation of adults to further study is vocational. The State spends more on vocational education than on any other form of post-initial study. Some of the most convincing work on adult learning done in the United Kingdom has been carried out in the context of vocational training. Yet, although the largest private sponsors of continuing education in Britain are commerce and industry, the effort they put into it is less than that of their counterparts in North America or the rest of Europe, and has been repeatedly stigmatized as insufficient. The NAB working party on continuing education concluded from its investigations that employers as a whole have no idea of what they want or need. With some important exceptions, mainly among large corporations, they are unable convincingly to defend themselves against the charge of inadequacy.

Even the case study published here, which comes from a company whose record in continuing education is much better than most, is open to the criticism that it says nothing about long-term planning, nor expresses a clear corporate policy. While such a situation exists, institutions engaged in continuing vocational education, including higher education ones, are seriously handicapped. The responsibility for taking action lies with companies, but for the most part their training personnel are either unconvinced of the need or too busy to meet it. Here would seem to be a research and consultancy role which higher education might play. Unfortunately British management, perhaps because of the anti-intellectualism of which it is accused, has hitherto shown itself less willing to open its activities to academic investigation than its competitors in the United States or Japan.

If this introduction appears to concentrate on the controversies surrounding the participation of higher education institutions in continuing education and on the gaps in knowledge about it, it will be clear from the following chapters that higher education already provides many opportunities for adult study and the institutions take their responsibilities in this sphere increasingly seriously. They are unlikely to do less in the foreseeable future if resources are available and only a shortage of means will prevent them from doing more, if they are to be believed. There is, it seems, no lack of demand. Certain ways ahead are suggested in the following pages, as well as obstacles to progress and deficiencies in knowledge. It is hoped and it is believed that this volume will inform people working in higher education, people in industry and commerce and the general public, all of whom have an interest in what higher education can do for continuing education. May it prove a useful basis for discussion, a stimulus to participation and open up avenues of inquiry.

# 2

# Provision and Need for Continuing Education

## *Gordon Roderick*

By the outbreak of the First World War a pattern had evolved in British universities that laid the main emphasis on undergraduate teaching, with postgraduate teaching playing a very subordinate role and research beginning to assume a position of increasing importance. It represented a fusion of the English 'model' of university life derived from Oxford and Cambridge, in which teaching and a close tutor-student relationship were pre-eminent, and the German 'model', in which the professoriate appointed for its research eminence was the ruling élite. In Britain, although the established professions of law and medicine had for long had an assured place at the ancient universities, there had been resistance to the introduction of newer professional studies, in particular the technologies. In response to the demands of the industrial revolution and intense foreign competition this had largely been overcome by 1914. The next period of change took place in the years following the Second World War, when the size of the university population multiplied greatly and further emphasis was laid on science and technology in response to the Cold War and to rapidly changing technology.

## The Robbins Report

The most significant document on higher education to appear in the United Kingdom was the report of the committee under the chairmanship of the late Lord Robbins, appointed 'to review the pattern of full-time higher education in Great Britain and in the light of national needs for resources to advise Her Majesty's Government on what principle its long-term development should be based.' It was published in 1963.

According to the Robbins Committee, higher education had four major aims:

1 Instruction in skills suitable to play a part in the general division of labour.
2 What is taught should be taught in such a way as to promote the

general powers of the mind. The aim should be to produce not more specialists but rather cultivated men and women. And it is the distinguishing characteristic of a healthy higher education that, even where it is concerned with practical techniques, it imparts them on a plane of generality that makes possible their application to many problems.

3 Advancement of learning and the search for truth.
4 The transmission of a common culture and common standards of citizenship.

Although the extent to which each principle was realized in the various types of institution would vary, 'ideally, there is room for at least a speck of each in all institutions....' In fact modern higher education is a marriage, sometimes an uncomfortable one, of a long-standing liberal tradition with the demands of economic utility.

## Post-Robbins Expansion

The Robbins Committee identified a number of factors which pointed to an increase in demand and called for a great expansion of higher education in the 1960s. In a statement which subsequently became enshrined as the 'Robbins principle' it declared that 'We have assumed as an axiom that courses of higher education should be available for all those who are qualified by ability and attainment to pursue them and who wish to do so.'

Since the Robbins Committee produced its report a transformation has been effected in British higher education, quite apart from the sheer massive expansion in student numbers. Firstly, the university system was strengthened by the creation of a number of new universities and the conversion of eight colleges of advanced technology into technological universities. Secondly, in the late 1960s, the Government created some thirty polytechnics out of existing technological institutions or amalgamations of various colleges. Finally, the public sector was further strengthened, in the 1970s, by the creation of new institutes or colleges of higher education.

The rapid expansion of the higher education system following Robbins, the apparent certainty in the increase in demand, the support for higher education by successive governments and oppositions appeared to herald a confident future for higher education. But a turnround was to come in the 1970s: firstly, as a result of a fall in the Age Participation Rate; and secondly, because of the introduction of a 'cash limits' approach to higher education in the light of what governments felt the country could afford. The Robbins principle was abandoned, and cash rather than qualified demand became the major determinant of the number of higher education places to be provided. Moreover, the Department of Education and Science predicted a fall of between 14% and 19% in total higher education demand to the end of the 1990s, because of demographic changes. Although many bodies have challenged these figures and conclusions, the Government has made it clear that, at least until 1987, its policy is to use the reduction in size of the 18-year-old age group as an excuse for reducing expenditure rather than for opening access to other categories of entrants.

# The Binary System

The British system of higher education is a binary one of two sectors: on the one hand the universities, on the other hand the polytechnics and other non-university institutions of higher education, which aim to be equal with universities but different. In spite of autonomy deriving from university charters, the independence of their teaching departments and the tenure-based security of their teaching staff, the university system is much more cohesive than might be expected. This is connected with dependence upon public finance, the peer-group system of academic validation, and the long-established corporate leadership of the Vice-Chancellors and Principals and the University Grants Committee. By the mid-1970s, the universities had collectively recognized the growing importance of 'all forms of continuing education both vocational and non-vocational' (UGC Report 1977-78) and they established a Continuing Education Record which identifies and defines continuing education in the university sector.

In the public sector, higher education is very different. Advanced further education, which is all education recognized to be above A level and which the DES regards for statistical and administrative purposes as synonymous with higher education, is distributed not only among the polytechnics and the institutes of higher education but altogether among some 400 colleges. The proportion of 'advanced' to 'non-advanced' varies enormously from institution to institution, which is significant, for the degree to which an institution does 'advanced' further education has great institutional and resource importance.

Polytechnics differ substantially in subject balance, as do the colleges; some have significant advanced provision outside of teacher training, some have substantial non-advanced provision, whereas others are mainly diversi-fied colleges of education.

Public sector institutions do not determine the level of their own courses, or validate their teaching or determine their priorities in allocation of resources, but they do have some freedom to take initiatives. In discussing the issue of flexibility with respect to the universities and the public sector in 1979 the DES observed: 'While the universities have shown remarkable capacity for expansion none of the responses to the discussion document *Higher Education into the 1990s* have suggested that the university sector is more flexible. The public sector has a long tradition of responding quickly to changes in perceived demand, monitoring and discontinuing courses at comparatively short notice.'[1]

The civic colleges of the late nineteenth century came into being as a response to the recognition of 'local' needs. But universities have long since ceased to be local centres or even regional centres. They have become instead national and international institutions catering mainly for the 18-24 year-old age group. This can be seen quite clearly in Table 2.1.

Thus 88% of the university population is full-time, compared with 80% at polytechnics. No fewer than three out of four of the student population at university are full-time, first-degree students. As only about 10% of first-degree students at universities are mature students (over 21 on entry) it follows that the great majority of university students are between 18 and 21 and studying for a first degree on a full-time basis.

| Universities | | | Polytechnics | |
|---|---|---|---|---|
| (a) Full-time | (b) Part-time | | (a) Full-time | (b) Part-time |
| 1 | 0 | Non-degree | 21 | 15 |
| 76 | 8 | First degree | 53 | 1 |
| 11 | 4 | Postgraduate | 6 | 4 |
| 88 | 12 | | 80 | 20 |

**Table 2.1**
Percentage of FTE Students in each Category.

The polytechnics appear to be rather better, though they may be accused of 'academic drift' in that they also concentrate too much on first-degree work and full-time education. But at the same time there is no complete overlapping of functions in that there is more part-time study in the polytechnics (albeit perhaps not enough) and there is non-degree work available in public sector institutions of which there is very little at universities. Our binary system therefore gives us a diversity of institutions. It is valuable in that one segment of higher education pulls in the direction of research and scholarship whilst the other pulls in the direction of local and regional social and industrial needs.

Successive governments have for some years, however, been concerned that the higher education system is not meeting the short-term and changing needs of industry and commerce. Too little attention, it is claimed, is given to the updating and training needs of industrial personnel.

# The Need for Post-experience Education

In recent years the need for post-experience education has been constantly reiterated by influential individuals and organizations. The Robbins Committee itself pointed to 'great extensions of knowledge in every field as making a three-year undergraduate course inadequate as the basis for training for many careers.' It went on to stress the need for additional training and stated: 'Some kinds of training are most appropriately taken immediately after the first degree: others may be more profitably taken after more years of experience in the world of affairs.... There will be an increasing need for this kind of training.... We consider the development of such studies at postgraduate level, particularly after the student has had some years of experience, to be a matter of urgent national importance.'[1]

A similar point of view was expressed by the Swann Committee in its report *The Flow into Employment of Scientists, Engineers and Technologists* (1968). It said that 'more attention should be given to education and training after experience of employment, and that post-experience students should form a rapidly rising proportion of the total postgraduate population: universities should come to regard as part of their normal provision post-experience courses for mature scientists, engineers and technologists.'[2]

The Russell Committee, although concerned with non-vocational adult education, drew attention to a type of adult education work in which universities should engage: 'Courses in new fields for professional or vocational groups including refresher and post-experience courses giving access to new knowledge or results of research.'[3]

More recently, in introducing a special one day conference on continuing education held in London on 1 May 1980 which was sponsored jointly by the Committee of Vice-Chancellors and Principals and the Universities' Council for Adult Education (as it then was), Sir Alec Merrison, chairman of the CVCP, noted that their recent submission to the House of Commons Select Committee on Education, Science and Arts had emphasized that the universities 'increasingly see their future in terms of part-time courses for people at different periods of life.' He also went on to say that 'the funding of universities makes inadequate provision for staffing continuing education courses.'

# What Continuing Education is provided

Details of their continuing education courses are returned by individual universities to the Universities Statistical Record at Cheltenham. USR subdivides continuing education courses into three categories according to the department responsible for organizing the course. The categories are: extra-mural courses (including joint courses with the WEA); postgraduate medical and dental courses; and 'other' courses. In 1981/82, universities in the United Kingdom organized 19,252 courses. Table 2.2 indicates the subdivisions into the three respective categories.

| Total Courses | Extra-mural courses | | Postgraduate | | 'Other' courses | |
|---|---|---|---|---|---|---|
| | No. | % | No. | % | No. | % |
| 19252 | 11,812 | 61.3 | 3,498 | 18.2 | 3,942 | 20.5 |

**Table 2.2**
Continuing Education Courses in UK Universities.

Continuing education statistics are broken down into nine subject categories: I education; II medicine, dentistry and health; III engineering and technology; IV agriculture, forestry and veterinary science; V biological and physical sciences; VI administrative, business and social studies; VII architecture and other professional and vocational subjects; VIII language, literature and area studies; and IX arts other than languages. In 1981/82 these groups accounted for 7.4% 21.2%, 3.4%, 0.4%, 11%, 21%, 2.6%, 10%, and 23% respectively of course provision. Oxford and London have a disproportionately large number of courses in Group II; if these universities are excluded from that group the proportion of course provision in it falls from 21.5% to 12%, the balance being fairly evenly distributed among other groups.

*It is of interest to note in passing that whilst one third of university continuing education is in languages, literature and the arts and one fifth in administrative, business and social studies, less than one twentieth is in engineering and technology.*

Although all subject groups no doubt contain some element of provision for the professions, the major contribution to professional post-experience provision may be assumed to be found in Groups I, II and III. In this context the surprising feature is the enormous variation in the provision of courses in Groups I, II and III as between comparable universities. Two universities of comparable student populations and faculty structure, for instance, have respectively 116 and 4 courses in Group I. Likewise, two comparable Joint Matriculation Board universities have 215 and 64 courses respectively in Group II and two comparable universities with prestigious engineering faculties have 34 and 5 courses respectively in Group III.

It may be that the key to these differences lies partly in the fact that some departments may not return Continuing Education Record forms for the courses they organize. However, assuming that incomplete statistics make only a minor difference, say of the order of not more than 10-20%, it does seem that some universities put greater effort into some subject areas than do others. No single university can be said to be strong in all three subject Groups I, II and III. The position for ten major universities in England is summarized in Table 2.3 (London, Oxford and Cambridge excluded).

| University | Total Courses in Groups I, II, III | % of total in Group I | % of total in Group II | % of total in Group III |
|---|---|---|---|---|
| 1 | 344 | 27 | 68 | 5 |
| 2 | 330 | 9 | 65 | 26 |
| 3 | 324 | 2 | 95 | 3 |
| 4 | 303 | 38 | 55 | 7 |
| 5 | 270 | 16 | 76 | 8 |
| 6 | 210 | 60 | 33 | 7 |
| 7 | 180 | 21 | 79 | 0 |
| 8 | 162 | 63 | 35 | 3 |
| 9 | 125 | 94 | 5 | 1 |
| 10 | 102 | 4 | 63 | 33 |
| Overall | 2,350 | 29% | 62% | 9% |

Table 2.3

*All the universities considered in the table have strong engineering faculties but engineering accounts for only 9% of the continuing education provision in Groups I, II and III* and there is great variability in the contributions to continuing education in engineering among the ten universities.

The differences in the contributions of the various universities to continuing education in the subject areas of Groups I, II and III may be related to special factors unique to a particular institution – this may be especially relevant to medicine – or to the ways in which departments are staffed or to the special efforts being made in particular areas: for example the creation of the Division of Continuing Education at Leeds or the appointment of an Industrial Liaison Officer in the engineering departments at Sheffield.

There are, as yet, (although plans are in train to produce such statistics) no comparable adequate statistics for short course provision in the public sector such as are available in the Universities Continuing Education Record.

An investigation was carried out in 1981 by David Wood as part of a project undertaken in the Centre for Research into the Education of Adults at Nottingham University and this contains useful information.[4] Table 2.4 indicates the distribution between full-time and part-time students in polytechnics.

|  | Enrolment | % of total | % over 25 |
|---|---|---|---|
| Full-time | 75,148 | 42.2 | 22.4 |
| Full-time sandwich | 40,248 | 22.6 | 11.3 |
| Part-time, excluding evening | 45,556 | 25.6 | 44.8 |
| Part-time evening | 17,140 | 9.6 | 67.7 |
|  | 178,092 | 100% | 30% |

**Table 2.4**
Enrolments in Advanced FE in Polytechnics in November 1979.

If these figures are compared with those contained in the UGC report on continuing education, two conclusions emerge. Firstly, that there are more part-time students in polytechnics and secondly, that there are more mature students.

The DES 'snapshot' figures of short full-time courses, writes Wood, cannot be interpreted meaningfully. The Committee of Directors of Polytechnics collects and publishes totals of enrolments on short courses in polytechnics without consideration of course length. These statistics show a progress from 25,000 enrolments in 1972 to 60,000 in 1979.

An internal CDP paper shows the following distribution between subject areas in 1978:

| | |
|---|---|
| Administrative and business studies | 23,000 |
| Engineering, science and technology | 19,000 |
| Education | 5,900 |
| Languages and other humanities | 5,000 |
| Other professional and vocational subjects | 5,300 |
| Social studies and allied subjects | 2,800 |
| Music, drama and visual arts | 1,350 |

# Administration and Organization

Much post-experience work is administered through the central administrative departments of universities, but a good deal of responsibility also rests with teaching departments. In many cases short courses are organized and administered by university departments established to deal with adult education (variously referred to as extra-mural, adult education, continuing education). Several universities even prior to the report of the UGC's Working Party on Continuing Education (which recommends such a step) were establishing boards of continuing education chaired by a senior university officer.

If liberal adult education is excluded from the provision made by universities, the major fields in which it is provided are medicine, teaching and technology. Postgraduate medical education depends mainly on the university schools of medicine, each of which has a postgraduate dean as organizer and administrator. Postgraduate medical education extends far beyond the provision made by universities for work towards degrees and diplomas. Postgraduate degree work in medicine in the universities is also post-experience. But it is only partly post-experience since the immediate postgraduate element in the training of doctors is designed to give them experience in which the knowledge and skills gained during initial training may be used.

Much post-experience work is done in teacher education, despite the running down of initial teacher training places and the abandonment of the area training organizations. The technologies cover a wide range of subjects and another area of considerable post-experience activity is business management. In addition to the special activities of business schools and management centres such as at Bradford, Cranleigh and Hendon, many universities also provide courses in these fields.

It has been pointed out that many universities have special departments responsible for adult education. The greater part of their work is in liberal adult education, although all provide some post-experience courses. In the past the majority of the teaching staff of such departments were funded according to a formula by which about 75% of their salaries was a direct grant from the DES whilst the remainder came from the UGC. The majority of these 'responsible body departments', as they are called, have no member of staff with specific responsibility for the promotion of post-experience work; in a survey it was revealed that only fourteen individuals have a full-time or part-time remit for organizing post-experience work. They included two DES-funded staff and two administrators, two deputy directors and two administrators; excluding these, and the special case of the Loughborough Centre for Extension Studies, which has seven UGC-funded staff, there are no more than ten UGC-funded teaching staff spread over some thirty adult education departments who have a major responsibility for post-experience work. Yet the same survey showed that nineteen responses from twenty-four responsible body (RB) departments indicated the high total of 670 courses attended by 17,000 students. The total volume of post-experience work provided by all member departments of the Universities Council for Adult and Continuing Education (UCACE) must be considerably in excess of these figures. This is achieved by some 340 RB-funded staff, even though they are appointed for other purposes and have a variety of commitments both to the DES and to their own universities, and by the dozen or so individuals identified in the survey.

In his survey of polytechnics, Wood reports that several have working parties, standing committees or simply staff groups or a 'tutor in charge' who are responsible for continuing education or recurrent education or adult and continuing education. Others which may not yet have formally established machinery have, nevertheless, plans to increase continuing education activities (ie by short course provision, assistance and encouragement to enter students to higher education, and the strengthening of links with local industry, professions and the community).

In the public sector the growth of short courses is a major aspect of the growth of continuing education. Wood reports that 'the administrative system of further education is designed to serve the teaching of registered students on approved courses measured in years and annually repeated'. Short courses have been recognized in the system by their specifying maximum but not minimum lengths. A short course may be 'poolable' if it is recognized as advanced further education, or 'rate supported' if it is non-advanced or alternatively 'self-financing'.

All colleges make provision for short courses (which on the whole seem to be a matter of departmental or individual initiatives). Several have established some form of short course unit which may be responsible for all the institution's work or in some cases for that of a few departments only. Short course units provide administrative support for departments and staff who are planning, marketing and running their own short courses.

The major fields in which the polytechnics and other major colleges operate short courses are in management studies and in applied science and technology. 'On the basis of the evidence of prospectuses their programmes of short courses in these fields do not seem very different from those of the universities, and especially the technological universities.'[5]

Dr George Tolley, formerly director of Sheffield City Polytechnic and later director of Open Tech, in a speech entitled 'Mid-Career Education: the priority of the 1980s' given at a special national conference on continuing education organized by the British Association for Commercial and Industrial Education (BACIE) in May 1982, summarized the public sector's contribution to post-experience education in the following words: 'Some good work is already going on in the colleges, some of it very good, but there is not enough of it, it is not well enough known, and it is being done under difficulties which could be, or should be, lessened.' He went on to say,

> If long courses leading to qualifications and in-service provision for teachers are excluded, there must be very few polytechnics and colleges that devote more than 1% of their teaching and other resources to the mid-career needs of those in employment. Is that adequate and is it reasonable? I would say not and I would say this for a number of reasons. Firstly, because educational institutions that have a particular responsibility for meeting the needs of local industry ought surely to have much more than a peripheral involvement in updating and retraining personnel. Secondly, for polytechnics in particular, there are national needs also to be met which justify commensurate allocation of resources. Thirdly, there remain many opportunities for extending provision.

The reason why continuing education remains a marginal activity of higher education have been discussed by the UGC and NAB working parties (see Chapter 10). For Dr Tolley the problem was primarily one of attitude. He referred to the public sector, but his comments apply equally well to the universities:

> Why is it that in resource terms the provision of mid-career opportunities is so peripheral? Firstly, the question of attitudes of staff in colleges. That full-time courses in polytechnics have 25% of mature students whereas universities have only 8%, tells us something about the excellent job polytechnics staff are doing, but does not alter the fact that the priorities throughout the whole of post-school education have been identified with full-time provision of long courses leading to national qualifications. The internal organisation and management of polytechnics and colleges, the composition of peer groups, the criteria for recognition and advancement, the machinery for selection and assessment of students, the methods of marketing courses – all those things reflect the overwhelming preoccupation with full-time courses and have deeply influenced the

culture of the educational community, including the attitudes of staff. Many staff, therefore, regard the provision of opportunities for those in mid-career employment as both optional and extra to their prime commitment to what they feel happiest (and more secure) with, ie long courses that are firmly based within the educational institutions with the decisions of selection, progress and assessment of students firmly in the hands of teachers.

## Financial arrangements within Institutions

Complex financial procedures are a bar to the promotion of short-course work both in universities and the public sector. The position is further bedevilled in the public sector by local authority accounting procedures.

Wood in his survey of public sector colleges found that 'Short-course provision is an entrepreneurial educational activity involving substantial risks, rather uncertain rewards, and in some situations, fierce competition' (p. 21).

In universities there is very considerable post-experience education in medical faculties and schools of education. But here organization, administration and funding are on different bases from those in the remainder of the university sector. In most universities, extra-mural departments or departments of adult education make a substantial contribution to post-experience education in liaison with internal departments. A survey by a UCACE working party was made of the financial arrangements extra-mural departments adopted to conduct such work.

It found that post-experience courses are organized on the basis of payments to teaching staff, usually at the extra-mural rate, but in some cases at rates that are negotiated with teaching staff contracted for the courses. These costs are recovered from the students through fees. Only in about half the replies was it indicated that a charge was made to students to cover the time of the organizers and promoters of courses.

All departments, in assessing the student fee, covered direct costs such as publicity and promotion, visual aids and materials and residential accommodation. No direct charges were made for teaching accommodation, cost of offices, heating, lighting and use of telephones, but in many departments these would be subsumed in a general 'university overhead charge' which varied from as low as 10% to as high as 40%.

The fee for a particular course was estimated in relation to such direct costs as those above plus overhead charges, but with a view to achieving a suitable 'profit', bearing in mind a realistic assessment of the market response for that course.

A pattern emerged as to what happened to the surplus balances, ie excess of income over expenditure for all the courses at the year end. Some departments remitted the whole of the balance to their university, whereas others retained the complete amount. Yet in other cases a proportion of the balance was retained – this could be from 10% to 50%. Likewise, the distribution of 'profits' between the organizing department and a co-operating internal department varies from university to university and within a university from course to course. Some extra-mural departments retain all the profits whereas in others a quarter, a half, or some other agreed fraction goes to the co-operating department.

Clearly, arrangements are ad hoc and variable. There is evidence of the 'risks' and 'fierce competition' Wood discovered in the public sector. As in many cases 'profits' is the motivating spur, one can legitimately ask whether certain areas of client 'need', where profit returns are marginal, may be neglected in favour of other areas, perhaps of lesser need, but where clients are able to pay the sums required to provide profits for all concerned.

The UGC Working Party on Continuing Education recognized the need to put financial procedures on a sound and positive footing. It recommended that 'arrangements for the retention of fee income ... should be designed as far as possible to encourage initiative' (para 7).

## The Status of Continuing Education

How is continuing education to acquire 'status and recognition equal to research and to the traditional teaching of young undergraduates' (UGC Working Party Recommendation (a))? In the days when universities were far more autonomous than they are today, research took a long time to become a recognized and accepted part, and one need only think of such nineteenth-century figures as Faraday, Joule, Mendel and Darwin to realize that even in the sciences much of the best research was conducted 'outside the walls'. But there is a greater urgency in the need to gain recognition for continuing education. Professor Richards in an address at University College, Cardiff, put his finger on it:[6]

> The unwillingness of many universities, or rather of many people in universities, to make even small changes is hindering the natural need for local initiatives to meet local community requirements and changes in educational patterns, and is forcing upon us national edicts which are not wholly acceptable.

There have been few attempts made to define a strategy and to argue through constructively what the continuing education of a university as a whole should be and to plan effectively in the light of that. A working party at a major university – incidentally one that is most active in post-experience provision – comments: 'The present organization of continuing education in the university is confused and confusing – it does not encourage the full use of existing resources nor facilitate new initiatives.' There is clearly a need within each university for a top-level body to co-ordinate all the continuing education activities, to provide a forum for discussion, and to consider the appropriate share of resources to be devoted to continuing education. Also, to examine the special problems for the development of post-experience work caused by existing staffing and administrative procedures and to formulate proposals to overcome them.

The same arguments, of course, apply to the public sector institutions, although many of those with short course units may be better placed to promote post-experience work than the universities. However, Dr Tolley in his BACIE speech argued that: 'Some deep-seated attitudes and practices have to change if there is to be anything in the nature of a significant shift in resources or interest.'

The spur to that change must come, argued Dr Tolley, from outside institutions:

> The future education service is faced with a multiplicity of demands and pressures. It cannot respond with equal vigour to all demands. Higher education also is facing a variety of needs and demands and its resources are being severely cut back. The Government must give a lead on priorities, and one of these priorities must be that of securing adequate provision for the re-tooling of the nation's technical and professional manpower.

## The Skills needed to promote Continuing Education

The promotion of post-experience work requires a variety of skills: the identification of needs, negotiation with clients, the design of courses, the promotion and marketing of course programmes. Anyone who is concerned with the recruitment of staff for the promotion of continuing education will be only too aware of the paucity of academic entrepreneurs in our higher education system who have the necessary skills and experience.

The DES discussion paper *Post-experience Vocational Provision for those in Employment*, whilst rightly drawing attention to the need for in-service training of staff for post-experience work, did not spell out in detail the many different kinds of tasks involved, and there seemed to be an implicit assumption throughout it that all the tasks may be carried out by the same person from the moment the idea of a course is first mooted to the teaching and final course evaluation. Whilst at present this is largely the case in Britain it may not be in the future and maybe we can learn here from North American practice.

In the United States those involved in the promotion of post-experience courses are best described as continuing education 'professionals'. They will have been drafted in, not only from higher education institutions, but also from industry and commerce. They act as a team, bringing to the task all the skills required, including the application of cost-effectiveness to the programmes and operations. Not all of them are 'academics' in the conventional sense of having been appointed on the basis of academic scholarship. Nor are they necessarily expected to demonstrate an expertise in some area of purely academic scholarship (though many of them do) and their promotion is not linked to academic research and teaching. The total activity is seen as one embracing people with a variety of complementary abilities and thus programme managers and organizers are able to call on individuals with expertise in financing and accountancy, computer skills, promotion and marketing, educational methodology and guidance and counselling.

We in Britain are some way short of the American model of a blend of academics and other 'experts' working together as a team, and it may not be a model we would wish to adopt. Nevertheless, there should be greater incentives created for our academic staff to become involved in continuing education, among which a fundamental one should be reconsideration of the criteria for promotion, for, at present, involvement in continuing education leads to little or no advantage with regard to the promotion prospects of an individual. There is a need therefore for adequate recognition of calls on staff time in the provision of post-experience courses when drawing up staffing procedures, salary scales, conditions of service and staff training and development.

## Who Pays?

The Government, through the UGC and the DES, have stressed the paramounting of the 'self-financing' principle as a guideline – the UGC in 1981 with regard to continuing education and the DES with regard to Pickup.

In its 1980 discussion paper the DES stated:

> Since both employer and employee stand to gain from the enhancement of the employee's capabilities through such provision, it is a basic feature of the Government's approach to its further development that with some exceptions of principle or detail, the beneficiaries, and not the State, should meet the full costs involved. In practice, since an individual's willingness to undertake continuing education will benefit his employer, if not immediately then in the longer term, and will be influenced by that employer's readiness to release him as appropriate, and meet most, if not all, of the fees charged, the cost burden will fall largely to the employer. (para. 4)

However, the paper also stated that the DES would 'make available some limited advance funding to "pump-prime" new developments or underwrite the element of risk involved until it could be repaid... when fee income was available.' This attitude seems unrealistic and demonstrates a lack of understanding of what full-cost, self-financing would imply in terms of charges to clients. When the new Pickup scheme was announced it transpired that £2m was to be allocated to the Open University and the FEU (Further Education Unit) Curriculum Review and Development Unit to support experiments in the development of new course design and planning techniques and teaching methods.

Within the university sector the UGC Working Party on Continuing Education have taken a much more realistic line than was taken by the UGC in its letter of 1 July 1981 to Vice-Chancellors and Principals. It abandons the self-financing principle and calls on the UGC 'to seek additional funds from Government in order to make an allocation in recurrent grant of approximately £500 per FTE PEVE student' (recommendation (c)). At the current level of work this would amount to a sum of some £2.5 m.

## Employers' Needs

All institutions of higher education, under pressure from central government, are giving serious consideration to continuing education; indeed it could be argued that many are anxious to jump on a 'bandwagon' that is already rolling under the impression that there is a great deal of money to be made. If everyone joins in and participates will there be profits for all concerned? This will depend on the ability of clients to pay but also on whether a free market of this kind based on competition to produce the best quality product at a low cost will necessarily meet employers' needs.

'Take up', according to the DES discussion paper, 'will depend on the employers and employees' perceptions of the appropriateness and cost effectiveness of the provision made' (para. 15).

The paper goes on to state that 'it may not be possible for institutions to meet small and highly specialised needs, unless similar needs can be identified over a wide range of employers. Where no appropriate means of co-ordinating demand exists, some local or regional clearing house or forum may need to be developed.'

In this connection more than one regional management centre has provided an analysis of regional resources for updating and training, and provides an information service for employers on those resources. Some polytechnics, too, have brought together employers and colleges into an active consortium for identifying needs and responses, and for pooling both ideas and resources.

In his BACIE speech Dr Tolley, in discussing this issue, said:

We need to know more about the needs and demands that have to be made through Pickup.... Two things are required to ensure an effective response. One is surveys that are based upon an analysis of needs of companies. It is at company level that needs must make themselves felt; it is at company level that these must be identified if there is to be effective commitment to action. ... Paper surveys will not work; people are going to have to sit down and to talk to each other, initially to identify the right questions before going on to attempt the right answers. ... Some forty or fifty field posts should be established to identify needs and resources to meet needs, and to coordinate and encourage a response from education and industry.

# References

1 Robbins, Lord (1963) *Higher Education: Report of the Committee under the Chairmanship of Lord Robbins* Cmnd 2145, pp. 101-102
2 Swann, M. (1968) *The Flow into Employment of Scientists, Engineers and Technologists* Report of the Committee on Manpower Resources for Science and Technology. Cmnd 3760
3 *Adult Education. A Plan for Development* (1973) HMSO, p. 73
4 Wood, David (1982) *Continuing Education in Polytechnics and Colleges* Department of Adult Education, University of Nottingham.
5 *ibid.*
6 Richards, E. J. (1975) *Adult Education: a Challenge to All* University College, Cardiff

# Further Reading

1 DES (1978) *Higher Education into the 1990s: A Discussion Document* February

2 DES (1980) *Continuing Education: Post-experience Vocational Provision for those in Employment* October

3 University Grants Committee (1984) *Report of the Continuing Education Working Party* January

4 Styler, W. E. (1973) *Post-experience and the Universities* Department of Adult Education, University of Hull

# 3

# The Organization of Continuing Learning in Higher Education

*Tyrrell Burgess*

## Common Nature of Higher Education Institutions

Academics typically overestimate the diversity of higher education. Working in one institution they notice most the differences in others – differences of size, age, structure, control, funding, modes of attendance, balance of levels of work and composition of the student body. It seems obvious that the University of Oxford with 15,000 students is a different sort of place from St David's College, Lampeter, with a few hundred. The universities of Scotland are all independent of each other: the university colleges of Wales are in a federation. Some institutions are collegiate, most are not. Some are on campuses, some dominate the centres of cities, some are spread about over several boroughs. There are institutions offering the complete range of subject disciplines and there are those specializing in one or a narrow group. Universities are chartered: polytechnics are established and maintained by local authorities. The former award their own degrees, the latter offer the degrees of the Council for National Academic Awards. Their sources and modes of funding are dissimilar.

Institutions differ too in the balance between levels of work (from undergraduate to doctoral) and modes of attendance (full-time, part-time, sandwich, short or correspondence courses). Some have a substantial research effort, others see themselves chiefly as teaching institutions. In some the students are mostly good at examinations, aged between 18 and 21, white and male. In others the students are more diverse, in age and educational and social background. Even the buildings may differ, from mellow courts to the most recent award-winning jerry-building. Any or all of these things will have an effect on the education of those attending the institutions, including those who are in some sense in continuing education. The question is how great the effect will be.

In the course of preparing a book about post-school education, I had occasion to contemplate that offered in a large number of diverse countries. Indeed part of the point of the book was a comparison of these differences.[1]

I came to the conclusion, however, that none of the very real differences was as important as the consistency of education the world over. From the point of view of the students the nature and practices of providing institutions were virtually identical. In short, what is done in educational institutions is not only consistent from place to place all over the world but has been so, I believe, since Aristotle. Young people in formal education attend lectures, seminars or tutorials. They read books, write essays for their teachers' judgement and watch demonstrations. They may carry out 'experiments' and projects. They may differ in the amount of individual attention they get, in the available choice of subjects or teachers and in the degree of initiative they may show. But everywhere the object of their activities is to cover a set amount of knowledge – the course, curriculum, syllabus – and then convince the examiners that they have done so.

# The Structure of Higher Education Institutions

The organization of study in this all but universal way depends upon a view of academic structure which is in turn based upon a particular view of knowledge. As for structure, this is how one vice-chancellor, Sir Robert Aitken, put it in a text book on university administration:[2] 'The Charter declares...the university...“shall be both a teaching and an examining university, and shall further the prosecution of original research in all its branches”. The branches of research, which are the branches of knowledge, determine the organisation of academic study.' The last sentence is extremely revealing.

In his university, like so many others, academic organization is divided broadly into faculties (of science and engineering; arts; medicine and dentistry; commerce and social science; and law) and then subdivided into departments. With their constituent departments the faculties form the framework of teaching and research 'and therefore of academic administration'. Organizationally a department is subordinate to a faculty and a faculty to the university senate. This subordination may be embodied in regulations. For example, 'the pattern of courses leading to a degree is often devised in a department, but requires the approval of the faculty and of the senate, whereas the content and the method of teaching of a subject-course are left to be decided by the head of the department, in consultation with his departmental staff.' The teaching activities of a department are co-ordinated by the faculty, since a given student may be taught in more departments than one. The examining activities of a department are regulated by the faculty and the senate, in the interests of 'reasonably uniform standards'.

Sir Robert also offers this interesting contrast: 'Even problems of the timetabling of classes sometimes have to come to the Senate to be settled. By contrast, the research activities of a department are almost entirely its own affair; they are determined by the interests and ideas of the head of the department, and his staff (with his approval)....' Could even fiefdom go further? The central activity of research is independent: there is horsetrading over timetables.

Most teaching and research programmes can fit into and be administered in this framework, says the vice-chancellor, but a few *refuse to conform* with it.

(His italics.) The solution is the extra-faculty department. Administrative problems also appear with degree courses taught in departments in more than one faculty: they are met either by cross-membership of the faculties concerned or by the establishment of joint boards or committees.

Departments are headed by professors to whom their staffs are responsible. Larger departments may have two or more professors, each responsible for teaching and research in a division of the subject, each with his academic staff. Departments not only grow, they divide. Sometimes a completely new department is formed, its subject forming a separate new degree programme. Sometimes new departments, separate for their administration and postgraduate work, remain associated in a 'school' for undergraduate teaching. There are also 'personal professorships' – for professors, so to speak, without portfolio. All professors, in Sir Robert's university, were members of the senate.

## Resistance to Change

This kind of academic organization, which is largely unquestioned in higher education, is both more recent than many academics think and more resistant to change than some hope. Jencks and Riesman[3] date its origins in the United States to the 1880s:

> This was...the period when national learned societies and journals were founded and when knowledge was broken up into its present departmental categories ('physics', 'biology', 'history', 'philosophy', and so forth), with the department emerging as the basic unit of academic administration.

Similar features can be seen in the civic universities in Britain in the same period, and both were influenced by the Humboldt reforms in Germany.

Its resilience derives from the combination of unquestioned academic assumptions and established academic bureaucracy. Against this combination innovators have retired baffled. In one of the earliest international studies of 'interdisciplinarity'[4] J. R. Gass concluded that the reason why universities were conservative in what and how they taught lay in the fact that academic disciplines were the basis for the organization of knowledge for teaching purposes: 'The disciplines are not only a convenient breakdown of knowledge into its component parts, they are also the basis of the organization of the university into its autonomous fiefs, and of the professions engaged in teaching and research.' To meddle with the disciplines, he concluded, was to meddle with the whole social structure of the university.

At about the same time Harold Perkin studied the 'new maps of learning' appearing in the clutch of new universities established in Britain in the 1960s specifically to encourage innovation.[5] He concluded:

> Within this freer structuring for growth we have seen that the cellular or collegiate system offers more flexibility in social organization, the schools system more in academic organisation. Neither system, however, has

completely overcome, nor perhaps should it, the tendency towards departmentalism which is both the strength and the weakness of the academic profession.

His solution was that

for the health of the university system, to prevent hardening of the academic arteries and stagnation of the scholastic and scientific bloodstream, there ought to be once in every generation the founding of a wave of new universities as numerous and experimental as those of the United Kingdom in the 1970s.

Nothing could better have summed up the subject departments' resistance to change than the stated conviction that the only remedy is to start again every generation with some new institutions.

The OECD study already quoted came to equally sombre conclusions. The causes of failure to encourage interdisciplinarity included inadequately defined goals; rigidity among teachers, especially professors, 'who all too often cling to their lecturing role and remain cloistered in their discipline', fearing challenges to their discipline or their status; absence of individual or collective leadership over the teachers and over those institutional means which make a team experiment possible; difficulties of coherence and of avoiding a simple juxtaposition of disciplines and the encyclopaedic approach; resistance of the traditional structures at all levels – separations among disciplines, examinations, diplomas, jobs for graduates; disarray of students faced with confused, incoherent and arbitrary teaching and the lack of any professional goal; operational difficulties of scheduling, budgeting and the like. 'In summary, there were problems involving goals and curricula, problems involving personnel, problems involving institutions, problems involving facilities.'

It is impossible not to sympathize with the academics who resisted innovatory demands which went against the grain. It is also easy to see how students became confused when an organization of learning was attempted which was inconsistent with the whole structure of academic institutions. On the traditional view of knowledge and learning the academics were and are undoubtedly right to be distrustful of innovations which seem to attack subjects and disciplines. Human knowledge has been hard won, and attempts to teach without the traditional framework seem remarkably like attempts to teach chaos. All the normal pre-occupations of academics – with the demands of the subject, with concern for the level of studies in higher education, with the defence of standards and the pursuit of excellence – are bound up with an entirely defensible conservatism in the face of the unknown. The most familiar description of the task of higher education is the preservation, extension and dissemination of knowledge – to which it is often added 'for its own sake'. It is a noble aim, and attacks upon it must seem like barbarism.

## Incompatibility with Demands of the Outside World

It is important to realize, however, that this view gives rise to some implicit assumptions which are general among academics and rare elsewhere — because this realization has important consequences for continuing education. The academic assumption is that there are organized bodies of knowledge which are understood by some people (professors, and to a decreasing extent assistant professors and lecturers of various grades) and passed on to others (the students). The teachers possess something which it is their duty to impart: their job is to initiate the young into their mystery.

People outside academic life make quite different assumptions. Individuals see education as something that will help them to improve themselves and their life chances. Governments look to education to cure social and economic ills, from football hooliganism to unemployment or skill shortage. Employers seek from it a selecting device, specific training and a help in their technical or managerial difficulties. The starting point for most people outside education is not subjects but problems. They wish to overcome ignorance, incompetence and dependence as these evils relate to their lives not to academic disciplines. They wish to remedy the nation's resilient social and economic defects, or they wish to do a job or run a firm better.

The question is whether the organization of knowledge by subjects, disciplines, departments and faculties is apt for their purposes. There is no reason why it should be: it was established for quite different purposes. It is hardly surprising if education remains a permanent disappointment: it seems to promise so much and actually delivers so little. It is sad that there should be such a difference between the academic defence of higher education and the students' account of their experience.

## Inaptitude to meet Student Needs

Academics certainly claim to introduce students to a body of knowledge, but they typically claim more than that. They add that higher education inculcates a critical habit of mind and gives a grasp of underlying principles a higher priority than the mere acquisition of facts and technique. Graduates are asserted not only to understand their own subject but to show they can handle it, welcome what is new in it, explore it eagerly and work confidently on their own. Their rigorous intellectual discipline will have enabled them to collect evidence themselves and come to a balanced judgement. They will think for themselves and resist received opinion on the basis of reason.[6]

The students themselves typically report,[7] however, that everything in their courses tends towards the accumulation of knowledge and the acquisition of skill. They find that having the knowledge does not itself enable them to apply it. Even vocational courses are regarded as spurious because they seem to bring students no nearer the practice of their vocation. Students complain that their courses are overcrowded with detail, give little time to think, consist of tricks and dodges and of anything that could attract a twenty minute question in the final examination. These final examinations themselves often demand little more than memory. Others complain of narrowness and stultification. All ask for more control over their experience, through project work, options and discussions. Many demand more 'relevance', and a few seek to impose their own narrow relevance, as in 'black studies' or 'working class studies'.

None of this is to argue that no good ever comes of a higher education, rather that what good does come comes by chance. The organization of study, which is defensible in academic terms, is not apt for what students and society say they want. This tension, which is largely concealed by the predominance in higher education of young people straight from school, becomes particularly acute for those in continuing education. They, after all, have had some experience of the world outside the academy and come back to education, less to be introduced to someone else's subject than to find solutions to their own problems. Can there be any changes in the organization of study so as to ease this tension? This seems to me to be the most urgent question for higher education to resolve.

The key to its resolution lies in recognizing that the organization required by academics and that required by students are different and both legitimate. That required by academics has already been sufficiently described: it is to enable them to work on the problems of their subject or discipline in an organization of like minded people, with adequate intellectual leadership and proper defences against external control. Departments fulfil this function pretty well. They also suit that minority of students who know that they too wish to become academics and get to grips with the structure and problems of a subject or discipline.

Other students require something different, particularly those who return to education at their own or their employers' initiative. For them the introduction to a subject discipline as presented by its practitioners may meet their problems only tangentially if at all. Yet they may need the help which one or more subject specialists may give. For such students what is important is not so much particular facts, or even a particular ordered collection of facts, but method. It is method rather than information that gives mastery, and it is method that must be the chief business of education. By method I mean simply the way in which one diminishes one's ignorance, incompetence and dependence – not the technique of a particular discipline. There is no field of human interest, including subjects, which cannot be the basis for the mastery of method in this sense.

In so far as higher education involves the acquisition of skills and knowledge, the organizing principle must be their relation to the student's problems, not to the structure of the subject. It is a serious objection that to try to teach disciplines in an undisciplined way (as with 'interdisciplinarity' or modular courses) can lead only to chaos. But chaos can be avoided in another way: by making a programme of study a coherent educational solution to the problems of a particular student.

Many academics seem genuinely unable to comprehend this, as if there were no physics but that approached by existing physics courses. But physics has been different in the past and we can be sure it will be different in the future – may indeed be changing this very minute. Indeed the provisional nature of knowledge suggests caution in thinking of education as the accumulation of it. It is common for knowledge painfully acquired over time to become quickly out of date – and for the same fate to attend expensive refresher courses.

# An Alternative Organization of Study

The alternative organization of study can be based upon the initiative of each student. The curriculum will then be his curriculum, not one which presupposes purposes which are not his. Above all, the power relationships in higher education will be reversed. At present power lies with the academics who determine what the subject is and how it should be presented. They arrange, before students arrive, the course, curriculum, syllabus and the detail of timetables. The students take it or leave it.

If educational chaos is to be avoided through the organization of learning round the student's problems, the power and authority of academics will seem less inevitable. They will be less able, even (indeed especially) for the sake of instruction, to ask students to accept their greater knowledge, experience and wisdom. The faded idea of a community of scholars, which has hitherto seldom embraced students, could at last become a reality.

Academics also crucially wield the power of awarding success or failure – and do so in terms which cannot be apt for must students and their serious problems – hence student dissatisfaction with the form and content of final examinations. Instead, the tests for the efficacy of education can relate less to what the student knows than to what he can do. If education has been devised as a solution to his problems it is in principle possible to test how far the solution failed.

Perhaps the most important consequence of this approach for continuing education lies in its undermining of the exclusive principle of higher education. While such education is regarded as an introduction so some existing subject there is some justification for excluding those who do not know enough, or have too few years of previous education, or show no aptitude for it (though the grounds for these judgements have always been unsatisfactory). It may be right to exclude them, so as not to waste their time and demoralize them. Moreover, to admit people to an existing programme who are not likely to complete it successfully is the threat to standards that many academics fear. Such a threat does not exist if the intellectual coherence of a student's programme is rooted in the student's problems.

# Its Compatibility with Existing Structures

The question now is whether the learning of students can be organized in this way, without doing violence to the organization of subjects and departments. I believe that it can, and that there is enough experience already in higher education to suggest that it successfully can. This student organization would have five major elements: an extended occasion, which might be called a planning period, at the beginning of the course, in which the students prepare their own programmes; a means of ensuring the worth of the programmes thus produced; a personal tutor for each student; a departmental supervisor; and a means of accrediting the individual awards made at the end of the programme. It may help to say something more about each of these features.

During the planning period, which might last for perhaps six weeks, students would be asked to reflect seriously on what it is they themselves bring to higher education: their qualities, capacities, education and experience. This, after all, is what they have to work on. They can then be encouraged to say what problems (personal, vocational, academic) they mean to tackle and what more it is they expect to know and be able to do at the end of their programmes. They can then, with their tutors, prepare the programme which they propose to follow.

When education is individualized in this way, the checks and controls on the quality of education which are normally provided by curricula and syllabuses, are absent. Faced with this problem in the School for Independent Study at North East London Polytechnic, we created an external 'validating board' to maintain the sort of oversight of individual student programmes that the CNAA exercises over courses in polytechnics and other colleges.[8] This board under the chairmanship of Sir Toby Weaver, quickly evolved procedures for its work which included the scrutiny of a sample of students' programmes, meetings with students as individuals and in groups, discussions of its findings with staff of the school and the presentation of a chairman's report to the director of the polytechnic. In essence it was the task of the board not to determine whether an individual programme might or might not proceed (though it would certainly give advice) but to act as an external check on the judgement of staff in agreeing each student programme. As a consequence students themselves had the assurance that if they followed their proposed programme through to a successful conclusion they would have made good use of their higher education. Such success would merit the award of a qualification.

The planning and completion of a programme of higher education in this way is an onerous task for students, and it is important that they have consistent help. Each needs a personal tutor who will oversee his planning and progress and take responsibility for his academic work as a whole. Each member of the academic staff will have this tutorial responsibility – for students who may or may not plan to work in his particular discipline. In this sense the tutorial function is different from teaching: it is to help the student to organize his work, to keep to schedule, to overcome the inevitable difficulties – with work, facilities or colleagues.

The student's pursuit of study in an academic subject or discipline requires a different kind of help, one which is much more familiar in higher education – that is academic supervision. Some students whose programmes can be accommodated in one department may retain their academic supervisor for the whole of their programme. Others may have a succession of supervisors from a number of departments. To the familiar activities of supervision (guidance, direct teaching, assessment) the organization described here would add another: it would be the duty of each supervisor to mediate the requirements of the students' programmes to his department and discuss with his academic colleagues how they were to be met. This would clearly involve an element of negotiation to reconcile the proposals of students with the interests, capacities and specialisms of staff.

The last feature of a new organization of study, for continuing education, is the accreditation of awards. This becomes important when the normal safeguards of general final examinations are missing, because each student is being assessed individually. The problem is partly solved in traditional ways, through assessment boards with external examiners present. But there will also be the need to balance the judgement of tutors and supervisors who have had the prime responsibility for the student's work with that of a disinterested reader from within the institution itself.

The framework outlined here does not require fundamental changes in the academic structure of institutions. It does not abolish departments and faculties: indeed it uses them. What it does instead is to make it possible, within the academic structure, for students to formulate and solve their own educational problems through access to the ordered sum of available human knowledge. It represents an apt framework for the organization of learning in continuing education.

# References

1 Burgess, Tyrrell (1977) *Education after School* Gollancz and Penguin
2 Aitken, Robert (1966) *Administration of a University* University of London Press
3 Jencks, Christopher and Riesman, David (1968) *The Academic Revolution* Doubleday
4 *Interdisciplinarity* (1972) Report of a seminar organized by the Centre for Educational Research and Innovations and the French Ministry of Education. OECD
5 Perkin, Harold (1969) *Innovation in Higher Education: New Universities in the United Kingdom* OECD
6 See, for example, Mountford, James (1966) *British Universities* Oxford University Press
7 See Beard, Ruth (1970) *Teaching and Learning in Higher Education* Penguin
8 See Adams, Betty, Robbins, Derek and Stephens, Jenny (1981) *Validity and Validation in Higher Education* Research report and research papers 1, 2, 3 and 4 NELPCO

# 4

# Adult Learners in Higher Education

*Keith Percy*

## Definitions

In discussions of higher education and continuing education there are immediate difficulties in making a logical start by attempting to establish the facts. Statistics are collected according to varying definitions; there is much that we do not know; and there is much that is unknowable.

Legally, almost all students in higher education are adults but, clearly, the concern here is with students who have not entered higher education directly from school. The chronological age definition of 'mature student' varies from one higher education institution to another and from one statistical table to another. It may be 21, 23 or 25 years and may be age on entry or current age. The Advisory Council for Adult and Continuing Education (ACACE), in seeking to make a distinction between 'initial' and 'post-initial' education, emphasized the qualitative difference in the educational experience of those adult learners who return to the educational system after a 'substantial break'.[1] Such a concept is too indeterminate to be used in the collection of statistics but serves well enough to indicate the focus of this chapter.

A definition of higher education is almost equally problematic. The Department of Education and Science defines higher education to include all 'advanced' courses – which means those held to be post-A level. However, most information sources and most policy discussions about adult learners in higher education relate primarily to universities, secondarily to polytechnics and only latterly and incidentally to other public sector institutions. Tables 4.1 and 4.2 (below) show the injustice done to colleges in the public sector, which provide significantly for mature students, by this situation. However, because of the level and range of their advanced courses and because of the symbolic power and educational prestige which they enjoy, universities and polytechnics are the objects of most policy and research attention, and this chapter to a considerable extent necessarily follows that bias. Discussion of adult learners in higher education – as defined above – is here concentrated upon adults in:

a   Full-time and sandwich first-degree courses
b   Part-time first-degree and diploma courses
c   Courses organized by university extra-mural departments
d   Post-experience vocational education and other short courses (including Easter and Summer schools) organized in universities (not necessarily by an extra-mural department) and in further education
e   Other modes of access to higher education learning facilities such as 'open lectures' schemes, *ad hoc* auditing of parts of courses, independent study, etc.

Adults studying for postgraduate degrees and diplomas are largely not considered in this article (there is little separable data and, by definition, all postgraduate students are older). Adult students on advanced, but not degree courses in further education are also referred to only incidentally.

|  |  | All students | Aged 25 or over | Comments |
|---|---|---|---|---|
| a | Full-time/sandwich undergraduates in universities | 175,931 | 11,173 | Mature=6.4% of total |
| b | Full-time/sandwich undergraduates in FE | 60,992 | 7,443 | Mature=12.2% of total |
| c | Part-time undergraduates in universities[1] | 492 | Unknown but probably majority | Part-time=0.3% of all degrees |
| d | Part-time undergraduates in FE | 5,571 | Unknown but probably majority | Part-time=8.4% of all degrees |
| e | Birbeck undergraduates | 1,139 | Unknown but probably majority | 93% are part-time |
| f | Open University undergraduates | 43,792 | Approximately 40,000[2] | – |
| g | Open University associate students | 2,549 | Approximately 2,000[2] | – |
| h | Students on initial teacher training at colleges of education | 82,369 | 15,548 | Mature=18.9% of total |
| i | External students in the UK registered 'privately' with the University of London | 9,113 | Unknown but probably majority | – |
| j | Full-time students in FE on advanced but not degree courses | 44,932 | 14,951 | Mature=33.3% of total |
| k | Sandwich students in FE on advanced but not degree courses | 16,458 | 2,352 | Mature=14.3% of total |
| l | Part-time day students in FE on advanced but not degree courses | 76,237 | Approximately 30,000 | Mature=40% of total[2] |
| m | Part-time evening students in FE on advanced but not degree courses | 33,166 | Approximately 22,000 | Mature=60% of total[2] |

[1] Excluding Birbeck and the Open University
[2] The proportion aged twenty-five and over was taken from 1976-77 figures as this data was not available for 1975-76

**Table 4.1**
The Distribution of Adult Students in Higher Education in England and Wales: 1975-76.

# Data

Table 4.1 usefully summarizes the involvement of adult students in a variety of forms of higher education in 1975/76. It is taken from Woodley 1981[2] and is a combination by him of a range of tables in Wynne 1979[3] and the DES Statistics of Education for the relevant year. It is a difficult table to bring fully up to date from published sources, partly because Wynne relied on some private communications, but more importantly because some details which enable mature students to be identified have been omitted from later officially published statistics, and because of the use of age 25 or over as the definition of adult students.

Woodley comments on Table 4.1:

> The bulk of older students ... were with the Open University or they were taking advanced but non-degree courses in the further education sector (categories j-m). In numerical terms the universities offered more places on full-time undergraduate courses to older students than did the further education sector, but the proportion of older students was much lower. The further education sector, on the other hand, offered far more part-time undergraduate opportunities than the universities and it seems likely that, in total, the two sectors catered for an equal number of older undergraduates.[4]

These comments seem as likely to be valid ten years later as they did in 1975/76. In 1978/79 adults aged 25+ were 6.3% of the full-time/sandwich undergraduates in universities in England and Wales.[5] Table 4.2, which refers to Great Britain and excludes the Open University, does indicate a 50% increase in the number of part-time students on university under-graduate degrees between 1978/79 and 1983/84. Nevertheless, in the latter year there were only 5,600 part-time undergraduates, only 2.3% of the full-time total (cf Woodley's figure of 0.3% for England and Wales, excluding Birkbeck College, in 1975/76) and interestingly only two-thirds of this part-time total were reported as studying for a qualification.

| | Thousands | | | % Change since | |
| --- | --- | --- | --- | --- | --- |
| | 1978/79 | 1982/83 | 1983/84 | 1978/79 | 1982/83 |
| Full-time/sandwich undergraduates | 239.2 | 250.0 | 244.2 | 2 | −2 |
| Part-time undergraduates | 3.8 | 5.2 | 5.6 | 50 | 9 |
| Full-time postgraduates | 49.2 | 45.4 | 47.5 | −4 | 5 |
| Part-time postgraduates | 24.3 | 28.3 | 29.0 | 19 | 2 |

**Source** *University Statistics 1983/84* Volume 1

**Table 4.2**
Student Numbers in Universities (GB): 1978/79 – 1983/84.

Table 4.3, which also refers to Great Britain, shows total and adult (21+) enrolments in further education.

| | Adult (21+) Student Enrolments (Thousands) | | | | All Student Enrolments (Thousands) | | | |
|---|---|---|---|---|---|---|---|---|
| | 1979 | 1980 | 1981 | 1982 | 1979 | 1980 | 1981 | 1982 |
| Full-time | 94 | 94 | 100 | 100 | 184 | 187 | 204 | 218 |
| Part-time day released | 68 | 69 | 64 | 64 | 99 | 105 | 102 | 100 |
| Other | 8 | 10 | 18 | 21 | 8 | 11 | 20 | 23 |
| Part-time evening | 39 | 40 | 39 | 40 | 42 | 43 | 42 | 43 |
| TOTAL | 209 | 213 | 221 | 225 | 333 | 346 | 368 | 384 |

**Source**   *Statistics of Further Education 1982/83* Table 4

**Table 4.3**
Student Enrolments in Further Education (GB): 1979/1982 (Advanced courses only).

The table illustrates clearly that while adult students (21+) in 1982 were 45.8% of full-time students on advanced courses (degree and non-degree) in further education and 64% of day-release students, they were the overwhelming majority of students on part-time advanced courses – 92.3% on part-time day courses and 93% on part-time evening.

Using the same age definition (21+), Table 4.4 shows that, by comparison, 12% only of new university undergraduate entrants in 1982/83 were adult students (excluding, of course, the Open University). The table also indicates the distribution between subject areas of adult students in universities and illustrates their under-representation in agriculture, forestry, veterinary science, biological and physical science.

| | Number of UG entrants | | |
|---|---|---|---|
| | Mature | Total | Mature as a % of total |
| Education | 381 | 1,136 | 33.5 |
| Medicine, dentistry and health | 1,242 | 6,970 | 17.8 |
| Engineering and technology | 1,148 | 10,208 | 11.2 |
| Agriculture, forestry and veterinary science | 114 | 1,345 | 8.5 |
| Biological and physical sciences | 1,244 | 19,491 | 6.4 |
| Administrative, business and social studies | 2,347 | 17,176 | 13.7 |
| Architecture and other professional and vocational subjects | 194 | 1,058 | 18.3 |
| Language, literature and area studies | 988 | 9,295 | 10.6 |
| Arts, other than languages | 1,196 | 7,285 | 16.4 |
| TOTAL | 8,854 | 73,964 | 12.00% |

**Source**   USR reproduced from Appendix 5 of UGC Continuing Education Working Party Report, 1984

**Table 4.4**
University Mature Undergraduate Entrants: analysed by subject group: 1982/83.

A table reproduced from Jones and Williams for the earlier year of 1977 illustrates clearly the importance of penetrating behind global statistics on adult students to identify the patterns of behaviour of dissimilar subgroups.[6] Table 4.5 demonstrates a difference of subject interest between different age groups of adult university undergraduates. Over the age of 25, there is a sharp fall of enrolment in medicine, engineering and science; conversely education, social studies and the arts show a marked increase as the age range rises. Roderick et al. found similar patterns of enrolment with adult students in Sheffield University and Sheffield City Polytechnic.[7] '

|  | Age Group | | |
|  | 21-24 | 25-29 | 30+ |
| --- | --- | --- | --- |
| Education | 5.7 | 5.8 | 14.2 |
| Medicine and dentistry | 13.7 | 8.4 | 6.7 |
| Engineering | 25.3 | 15.9 | 5.3 |
| Agriculture and forestry | 1.2 | .8 | .6 |
| Science and maths | 16.2 | 13.0 | 7.1 |
| Social studies | 18.4 | 30.6 | 38.0 |
| Architecture and planning | 2.5 | 2.5 | .8 |
| English and modern languages | 8.3 | 11.4 | 13.9 |
| Other arts | 8.5 | 11.4 | 13.1 |

**Source**   Jones and Williams[6], based on USR

**Table 4.5**
Percentage of Students in Age Group, by Subject Group, of Full-time and Sandwich New Entrant Undergraduates to English and Welsh Universities: 1977.

As for the Open University, it has continued, of course, to grow significantly since 1975/76 (cf Table 4.1) and provides the great majority of part-time university first-degree places in the United Kingdom. Almost all of its undergraduate students are aged 21 and over. At the start of the academic year, February 1983, there were 66,403 OU undergraduates (provisionally enrolled, new and continuing students). Despite a somewhat hesitant development of community and post-experience continuing education since the mid 1970s, in the Open University in 1983 there were enrolled 7,367 associate students (engaged on degree-level courses not as part of a degree programme) and 12,805 students on short courses.[8] Table 4.8 below shows trends in the 1970s in detail.

Adult students enrolling with higher education institutions for extra-mural and short course work and the response to the post-experience vocational education initiatives made centrally, can be traced in Table 4.6.

|  | Number of Courses | | | | Number of Enrolments | | | |
|  | Extra-Mural Department | Extra-Mural/ WEA[c] | Other Departments | TOTAL | Extra-Mural Department | Extra-Mural/ WEA | Other Departments | TOTAL |
| --- | --- | --- | --- | --- | --- | --- | --- | --- |
| 1980/81 | 9,037 | 2,142 | 2,832 | 14,011 | 209,392 | 36,567 | 82,590 | 328,549 |
| 1981/2 | 9,531 | 2,240 | 3,583 | 15,354 | 222,939 | 37,437 | 100,738 | 361,114 |
| 1982/3 | 9,978 | 2,411 | 3,835 | 16,224 | 230,792 | 42,259 | 102,513 | 375,564 |
| 1983/4 | 11,158 | 1,932 | 4,107 | 17,197 | 253,764 | 32,599 | 117,730 | 404,093 |

a  Post-experience vocational education
b  Excludes postgraduate medical departments
c  Workers' Educational Association

**Source**   Universities Statistical Record and Universities Council for Adult and Continuing Education (UCACE) Annual Reports, 1981/82 – 1983/84

**Table 4.6**
Extra-mural, PEVE[a] and Short Course Numbers and Enrolments[b]: UCACE Universities, England and Wales: 1980/81 – 1983/84.

The table indicates an increase over a four-year period, 1980/81-1983/84, in university extra-mural courses (taken with extra-mural/WEA courses which suffered a net decrease) of 10.3% but a much larger increase of 45.2% in the short courses organized by other university departments which were largely, but not exclusively, post-experience vocational education. An increase (23.7%) in PEVE university courses can also be identified in the four-year period 1977/78-1981/2.[9] The UGC Working Party on Continuing Education calculated that, when converted to full-time student equivalents, PEVE university teaching in 1981/82 added up to about 5.6% of home undergraduate and postgraduate full-time student load.[10] It is generally assumed that the continuing education statistics are subject to vagaries of undercounting and overcounting according to the practices of the individual universities which make the returns. Subject distribution between institutions appears somewhat random. As an official statistician commented laconically:

> The number of ... (continuing education) courses run varies considerably from one university to another and has no direct relation to the number of degree students taught.[11]

Short course and post-experience work in further education is generally assumed to be substantial, although it is poorly recorded. However, in polytechnics alone in 1978/79, the DES reported an overall figure of 70,000 short course enrolments.[12]

Statistics which allow one to examine adult learners in higher education in their divisions and sub-categories are even more patchy and incompatible than the general figures. Yet it is important to look for indications of the age ranges, social class and sex composition, and minority group representation among the adult learner population.

With regard to age range, Table 4.7 shows clearly that the majority of university undergraduate adult learners (83%) are under 30 years on entry and, therefore, are not so very much older than the younger student. This observation accords well with most of the other evidence available – although there is bound to be considerable variation from institution to institution. In the early 1970s, for example, it was shown that in polytechnics the proportion of degree students aged 25 or over varied from 1% to 26%.[13]

The 'greying of the campus' has not yet become a phenomenon apparent in British higher education.[14] An NOP survey in 1982 found that only 0.5% of those over 55 are in full-time education in universities and colleges.[15] Similarly, in 1982 an Open University investigation demonstrated that the university had 2,700 older students (60+) who constituted 4.5% of its total undergraduate student body. These students, claimed the investigators, represented '90% of the older students believed to be studying in higher education (full and part-time) in the UK.' The older OU students were unrepresentative of their own age group and of the OU student body generally in that they had high previous educational qualifications. 11.5% of the over 65s already had one degree.[16]

A recent major national survey of mature student participation in a wide range of educational courses showed that one half of the mature students taking courses leading to qualifications were aged 30 or under and four out of five were under 41. Those on non-qualifying courses (these included

|  | | Age Group | | |
|---|---|---|---|---|
|  | | 21-24 | 25-29 | 30+ |
| Engineering | Men | 1,822 | 350 | 103 |
|  | Women | 80 | 12 | 4 |
| Science & maths | Men | 870 | 229 | 97 |
|  | Women | 351 | 67 | 46 |
| Social studies | Men | 929 | 428 | 436 |
|  | Women | 456 | 269 | 329 |
| English/languages | Men | 261 | 126 | 103 |
|  | Women | 365 | 133 | 178 |
| History/art | Men | 376 | 175 | 136 |
|  | Women | 261 | 84 | 127 |
| All Subjects | Men | 5,336 | 1,568 | 1,112 |
|  | Women | 2,178 (28%) | 706 (31%) | 897 (45%) |

**Source**   Jones and Williams, based on USR

**Table 4.7**
Entrants to Universities in England and Wales: 1977.

responsible body and local education authority classes) were older; one-third were aged 41-60 and one in five were over 60.[17] The National Institute of Adult Education 'Adequacy of Provision' survey carried out in 1967/68 comparably found that 29% of students in extra mural classes but only 17% of the population sample were in the age group 55 and over.[18] An investigation in 1979 into some 300 students in the Open College of the North West (an 'alternative to A levels' open access scheme specially for adults which gives a form of certification and, for increasing numbers, an access route into higher education) showed that the majority of students were between the ages of 26-45 years (59%) and only 5% were pensioners over 60.[19] By comparison, an investigation in 1980/81 into the eighty-nine members of the public attending the Open Lectures scheme at Lancaster University (through which individuals audited undergraduate lectures free of charge according to their own study interest) revealed that almost half were 51 years or over.[20]

Table 4.7 above suggested that there are different trends between men and women in terms of the age at which they may become first-degree students in universities. At the age of 21-24, one in four of the students were women; over 30, one in two were women. There is, of course, a relationship between sex of students recruited and subjects studied. Overall, using statistics relating to the 1970s, Wynne argues that 'adult women clearly do not participate in first degree studies at universities to the extent that younger women do'. While the percentage of female university undergraduates rose from 28% (1965/66) to 35% (1975/76), only 32% of students aged 25 or over were female in 1975/76.[21] The comparable figure for female first-degree students, age 25 and over, in further education institutions of higher education in the same year was only 26%.[22] Tight, in fact, writes of a 'demand from educationally poor qualified housewives ... for "fresh start" study opportunities on a part-time basis during the day, often leading to more formal undergraduate studies.'[23]

Social class bias in recruitment of higher education courses is well documented. For example, Embling observes that 'inequality, far from diminishing with the expansion of higher education and higher educational expenditure, has in many countries increased, for it is the non-manual classes which have exploited the extra opportunities.'[24] Thus, as Williamson summarizes, although in Britain manual workers are just less than half the employed population, in almost forty years new university students from manual worker backgrounds have risen from 2.1% to only 14.9%.[25] For all the rhetoric about the relevance and practicality of the polytechnic sector (and despite the emphasis on technical subjects), there is 'clear social bias in the level of courses for which students are enrolled, with students from higher social economic groups being more likely to be enrolled on full-time courses than other students.'[26]

There is no a priori reason why the social background of adult students in degree courses should differ from that of younger students. The empirical studies, such as they are, suggest that it is broadly similar.[27] Indeed, Hopper and Osborn's theoretical and empirical study is based on the perspective of continuing education as inextricably linked to the system of initial education in existing to correct its 'selection errors' and 'inefficiencies' (and thus confirming the existing stratification structures of society). If the initial education is viewed as concerned with the selection, job training, socialization and allocation to future life roles of two groups of young people, the mass of school-leavers (future manual workers) and the smaller élite of more academically able youngsters (future professional workers), then, urge Hopper and Osborn, degree education of adults may be viewed as operating to reclaim for élite training the mistakes of 11+ selection, grammar school drop-out, poor school teaching and individual circumstances.[28] It is a heavy (although persuasive) theoretical framework to build on a fairly small-scale empirical study of 112 adult students in first-degree courses in three universities and one polytechnic. However, there is some support for it to be found in the 1979 investigation of adult students in the Open College of the North West. Whereas only 5% of students were semi- or un-skilled workers, there was significant evidence of the adult who had been a grammar school 'drop-out', who had been initially successful but had been subsequently alienated by school experience, who was now attracted by Open College publicity to return to study.[29] A not unrelated piece of evidence is that McIntosh reports a higher proportion of Open University students as having had their schooling disrupted by frequent changes of school.[30]

Roderick et al. quote statistics from their research into adult first-degree students in Sheffield University and Sheffield Polytechnic and compare them with figures for the South Yorkshire area of the Open University. Whereas 21% of the adult degree students in the polytechnic and 33% in the university came from the professional and intermediate professions, 52% of Open University students came into these categories. The authors argue that the figures reflect the high proportion of Open University students who were (1978) teachers. 44% of the adult students in the polytechnic were in the skilled non-manual category (technical, clerical and service) compared with 30% in the university and 14% of Open University students.[31]

The social class analysis of the initial national intake of Open University students raised interesting social policy and research methodology questions. On the one hand, it seemed that the social class composition of Open University students was similar to that of degree students elsewhere in higher education (and thus the Open University was not attracting the 'working classes', as some commentators put it). On the other hand, students in other higher education institutions were being categorized by their parents' occupation. If the same criteria were applied to Open University students then their parental background (on the students' self reports) was similar to that of the adult population. Thus, 52% of Open University students' fathers were identified as in 'manual work' jobs and a further 28% in lower grade 'white collar' occupations.[32]

We have surprisingly poor information on the social class composition of extra-mural and short course students but they are generally assumed to be at least as middle-class as adult degree students.[33] Similarly, discussion of, say, ethnic minority adults in higher education must remain hypothetical for lack of data (although Appendix IV of Lucas and Ward (1985) lists thirty-two access courses in England 'with a particular emphasis on providing study opportunities for ethnic minority groups').[34] The comment of Little and Robbins is that 'the under-representation of black and brown students in higher education needs urgent quantification and analysis on a national scale; but it has been observed, and measures to correct it cannot wait on comprehensive research.'[35]

That comment might, in fact, be made generally. This section has underlined the uncertain nature of our knowledge of particular characteristics of adult learners in higher education, but what we do know is sufficient to indicate that provision and opportunities only partly match demand and need.

# Demand

Yet to talk of demand and need in adult education is to enter a minefield. The policy maker's apparently simple and reasonable question, 'what is the demand from adults for learning opportunities in higher education?' can be met only by complex and, perhaps, misleading answers. The most recent comprehensive 'attempt to measure broadly the overt demands and covert needs of the adult population for educational opportunities' observed that 'it is peculiarly difficult to study covert needs since many people may not be able to articulate those needs, particularly when they cannot perceive how those needs might be met.'[36]

The experience of the Open University is, however, indicative when considering adult learner demand. There was virtually no market research undertaken into demand for part-time degree opportunities at a distance prior to the establishment of the Open University; the decisions to establish the institution were based on political will and educational aspiration. Yet Table 4.8 shows the consistently high level of interest shown in the Open University throughout the 1970s. For every applicant accepted, there were at least one unsuccessful applicant and at least two other written inquiries. The three inquirers for each successful applicant who did not become Open University students all constituted an identifiable group of adults who had, in concrete form, expressed themselves as part of a potential demand for this form of higher education.

In 1973, the Open University investigated those inquirers who had not subsequently applied for a place and in 1977 those applicants who had declined a place offered to them.

| | Inquiries | Applica-tions | Available Places | Newly Registered Students | | Continuing Students | Total Students |
|---|---|---|---|---|---|---|---|
| | | | | Provisional | Final | | |
| 1971 | 123,556 | 43,444 | 25,000 | 24,220 | 19,581 | – | 19,581 |
| 1972 | 77,722 | 35,182 | 20,500 | 20,501 | 15,716 | 16,186 | 31,902 |
| 1973 | 71,757 | 32,046 | 17,000 | 16,895 | 12,680 | 25,744 | 38,424 |
| 1974 | 81,392 | 35,011 | 15,000 | 14,976 | 11,336 | 31,300 | 42,636 |
| 1975 | 109,858 | 52,537 | 20,000 | 19,823 | 14,830 | 34,528 | 49,358 |
| 1976 | 86,433 | 52,916 | 17,000 | 16,311 | 12,230 | 38,805 | 51,035 |
| 1977 | 75,541 | 49,956 | 20,000 | 19,886 | 14,971 | 40,156 | 55,127 |
| 1978 | 87,335 | 45,293 | 21,000 | 20,882 | 15,669 | 43,119 | 58,788 |
| 1979 | 81,783 | 42,754 | 21,000 | 20,719 | 14,995 | 45,968 | 60,963 |
| 1980 | 93,399 | 45,311 | 20,000 | 19,439 | 14,150 | 47,296 | 61,446 |
| 1981 | 84,051 | 43,004 | 21,000 | 20,338 | 14,478 | n.a. | n.a. |

**Note** The figure for inquiries includes only formal written inquiries received in the Admissions Office

**Source** Tight, based on *Open University Digest of Statistics* Vol. 1, Table 1[37]

**Table 4.8**
Inquiries, Applications and Registrations for Undergraduate Level Courses at the Open University: 1971/81.

Although responses must have been affected by post hoc rationalizations, in each case domestic and work circumstances on the one hand, and the range of courses and the nature of Open University teaching methods on the other hand, were mentioned by very substantial proportions of respondents as factors affecting their decisions not to proceed.[38] In other words, although very many of the 80,000 or so individuals who inquired in each year may be counted as part of potential adult 'demand' for higher education, 'demand' must be conceived of as multi-dimensional and multi-stage. Potential demand becomes real demand when the adult is prepared to make the changes to his or her life that participation will require and when that preparedness intersects with a match between what an institution offers and the adult's developing interests.

In the research into the adults of the Open College of the North West, a follow-up study demonstrated the fluctuations of 'demand' by those adults for higher education. Roughly one-third of the respondent students were firm in intentions to apply for a higher education place throughout the period of the follow-up study (20 months); a further third were similarly intent throughout not to apply. However, the remainder began by declaring that higher education entry played no part in their reasons for becoming Open College students but after a few months appeared to have 'gained confidence and adjust to a new and more positive self-concept.' Mostly, they no longer completely ruled out higher education entry as a possibility for them. Fifteen months or more later they had largely reverted to their earlier stance and no longer had any aspirations to higher education. Now, often, their reasons had changed. They had not lost their newly acquired academic self-confidence. Rather, the practicalities of effects on families and finances weighed heavily with them.[39]

The population survey conducted by the Advisory Council for Adult and Continuing Education in 1980 uses an interesting but debatable method of assessing adult demand for learning opportunities based on a combination of an individual's past record (if any) of post-initial education combined with his or her expression of wishes and aspirations. As a result the survey subdivides the adult population into eight groups and identifies two as the 'most promising "target groups" in which there is likely to be demand for continuing education.' The two groups account for 35% of the population. One group 'is rather younger ... contains more single people and is markedly lower in social class ... and ... is ... more inclined ... to want to study for work-related reasons. [The other group] is higher in social class ... Educational achievement is much higher ... and they are more inclined ... to want to study for non work-related reasons, such as personal interest.' The survey goes on to comment, with more sweeping self-confidence than its analysis justifies, that:

> potential participants in continuing education can be characterised broadly as falling into two types: working class people who want to improve their employment prospects, and middle class people who want to participate in general culture or follow personal interests.[40]

This generalization merits further examination in the context of higher education as well as elsewhere.

The ACACE survey talks freely of adult 'needs' but it does not, of course, simplify matters to substitute talk about adult wants, needs or interests for talk of adult 'demands'. In fact, it makes matters worse. One is then obliged, explicitly or implicitly, to make value judgements and priority assumptions on behalf of others – the educator determines that particular provision (normally paid for at least in part out of the public purse) is 'needed' by the adult or is 'in the interest of' the student.[41]

That is why, in fact, the provision of continuing education by higher education institutions is based on such an amalgam of conceptions and assumptions about the potential student, the market, social and individual need and what is educationally worthwhile. It is possible to derive from practice a whole range of approaches – some of which may be typified as follows:

*Traditional*
Continuing education provision is a given determined by past practice and the forms of knowledge.

*Passive*
Provision should be a response to what is asked for by those adults determined, confident and motivated enough to come forward to ask.

*Client-servicing*
Provision is tailored, at a cost, to meet the expressed requirements of client groups (eg employers).

*Marketing*
Any provision can recruit viable numbers as long as it is accompanied by high-profile professional marketing.

*Democratic*
Provision must depend on decisions in which student groups are involved (cf the WEA).

*Survey*
Provision should be preceded by surveys of public demands and needs.

*Curriculum development*
Provision should be rationally based on objectives derived from notions of the aims of the providers.

*Societal need*
Provision should seek to promote society's needs for appropriate technical, commercial, industrial and social expertise.

*Social progressive*
Provision should promote a more egalitarian and fair society and enable individuals to understand the mechanisms through which social change can be encouraged.

*Random*
Participation in provision is subject to fashion and unpredictability – it is worth trying most things once.

Evidently, a combination of the positive aspects of many of the above approaches must guide those involved in the provision of opportunities for adult learners in higher education. There remains, however, need for a linking philosophy or value framework for the practitioner which cannot be found in ill-fated simplistic attempts to gauge student demand or to judge student needs or in short-term (although worthy and necessary) developments to satisfy ad hoc client needs or the re-skilling requirements of new technology. Clearly, the continuing education activities of universities and polytechnics must stem from conceptions of the value and the range of university and of polytechnic education; from a notion that the quality of life for an adult in a society such as our relates to widely available access to learning opportunities by all sectors of the community; from an awareness that educational standards and levels increase from generation to generation through improvements to primary and secondary education and that, therefore, potential interest from adults in access to educational opportunities in higher education (but not necessarily in degree study) will commensurately increase; and from a professional expertise that understands that involvement by adults in educational provision follows after provision has been made, has been offered in the most accessible and convenient form, and has been brought to public attention by all the appropriate tools of marketing, awareness arousal, information and guidance, monitoring and evaluation.

# Access

Indeed, since the mid 1970s, there has been considerable development in removing 'barriers to access' (the metaphor which lies behind this phrase, which is in common use, merits consideration) between the adult and institutions of higher education.

With regard to flexible admission requirements, preparatory and pre-degree access courses, information, guidance and counselling, and credit transfer, one can indicate both a general movement of opinion and particular developments in the last ten years for adults wishing to take degree courses. Woodley, in analysing UCCA statistics on applicant and admitted adult students to first-degree courses observes that:

> a considerable proportion of admitted adult students had not met the normal entry requirements and this proportion increases with age.... The proportion of adults admitted without 'A' levels has increased over the last few years and ... those adults admitted with 'A' levels tend to have fewer passes and lower grades.[42]

> Nevertheless, Wynne emphasizes the variety of practice over admission of adult students between institutions of higher education, in particular in the application of non-standard entry regulations to adult applicants.[43]

Of course, as Wynne notes, implicit in most adult student entry regulations 'is the perceived need for evidence of ability to pursue a degree course successfully.'[44] The development of access courses and open college type schemes for adults (since pioneering efforts such as those at the City Lit. in London and the Open College Federation of the North West) to provide such evidence can be traced in the long listing contained in Lucas and Ward.[45] Similarly, after a lengthy gestation period during the 1970s, in which first the Open University and subsequently ACACE played the midwife, the desirability of a national network of local educational guidance services for adults has been taken over as conventional wisdom by the Department of Education and Science and its new development unit based in the National Institute of Adult Continuing Education. That coventional wisdom remains some distance from the achievement of such a network, securely resourced. In an associated manner, the development of bi-lateral and multi-lateral credit transfer agreements between the Open University and other institutions of higher education in the 1970s has contributed to an awareness of the value of credit transfer arrangements for adults wishing to upgrade their educational qualifications, to the Toyne Report[46], and to ECCTIS (the Educational Counselling and Credit Transfer Information Service),[47] but – because of the complexities and multiplicity of interests involved – a national scheme of credit transfer is a relatively remote ideal. On one of the major barriers to access for adults there has been no progress. The mature student grant for full-time degree study has declined in value; there have been no positive developments over the level of fees or the provision of grants for part-time degree students, and paid educational leave remains a matter for rhetoric.

However, developments in easing the access of adults to institutions of higher education, particularly to degree courses, beg the question of access to what? The development in universities other than the Open University of specially designed part-time first-degree schemes to fit the practical requirements of adults (eg involving evening and off-campus teaching) has been remarkably restricted. Extra-mural departments have been involved in some significant basic outreach or experimental provision, eg Liverpool's 'Second Chance to Learn' courses with inner-city working-class people[48] and Southampton's outreach project to a working-class housing estate[49]. But such innovations have not had results which have caused them to be replicated generally throughout higher education.

Indeed, although some extra – and intra – mural departments have developed sub-degree diploma work (to some of which adults can have access on a part-time basis), this kind of provision is not nationally available. Indeed, university teaching – certainly below postgraduate level – is almost totally monopolized by the format of taught courses leading to degree awards. It may be permissible for an adult to take parts of courses for interest without the intention of achieving a degree, but such an involvement would be abnormal, isolated and require special arrangement. Yet to make such an arrangement easily possible and legitimate would more nearly match the life situation and expectations of many groups within society – for example, the unemployed and the older person. Polytechnics, which frequently have modular structures, could adapt to such provision even more easily than universities.

Deliberate policy decisions by institutions of higher education to examine ways in which their educational facilities and expertise could be made accessible to identifiable significant groups in society which may be under-represented in higher education – older people, ethnic minorities, women, the unemployed, the rurally isolated – are uncommon. However, to concentrate institutional attention in such a manner on 'target' groups would not – one may argue – necessarily mean abandoning any concept of what is 'appropriate' for a university or a polytechnic to do or to provide. But it would require interpreting that concept flexibly without identifying it absolutely with past practice – for example, with degree and conventional extra-mural work, with courses, certification and enrolments and with locations, academic terms and face-to-face teaching. It seems possible that universities and polytechnics could be perceived as resources for learning to be used variously by adults in their locality through such means as auditing lectures, summer schools, associated University of the Third Age groups and assistance by higher education teachers with individualized learning projects.[50] The point is that none of these means would require outrageous additional resource and ought, therefore, to be politically and pragmatically possible.

# Experience

Neave claims rightly that:

> once an institution ... throws down the structural and qualificatory barriers associated with entry to higher education, it merely reveals the fundamental social-structure barriers that lurk beneath the more ostensible pedagogic hurdles.[51]

Certainly some have argued that not only is it necessary to give adults different means of gaining access to higher education but also – in order to treat them fairly – that their adulthood implies that they will need to be dealt with separately as a group, that special support will be necessary and, even, that curriculum and teaching ought to be adapted and adjusted to be appropriate.

Certainly, the practicalities of the situation of the adult student in degree study imply provision of married accommodation, creches, financial loan arrangements, and counselling services. The experience of many institutions has suggested the desirability of, on the one hand, social occasions organized specially for adult students and, on the other, study and examination skills courses and workshops in which the overriding aim is to boost the adult learner's confidence.[52] Nevertheless, there have been a range of investigations which show that the degree performance of adult students compares favourably with that of younger students. Woodley summarizes a variety of studies thus:

> the maturity associated with increasing age and experience seemed to be a positive predictor of success for some arts and social science courses. The general finding [was] that older students do better in arts and social science and worse in science and maths.[53]

It is important to ask, however, if there is evidence that adults learn differently or less effectively than younger students or if they need to be taught by special methods. Certainly adult students talk about defective memories; extra-mural tutors suggest that adults should be taught through discussion methods; and institutions such as the Open College of the North West are advertised as 'a new approach to part-time learning for adults.'

Questions about adult learning do not, however, permit many generalizations. For example, one might expect similar ranges of difference between students over 21 on measures of personality, orientation, aptitude and preference for informal teaching as have been found between students in higher education aged between 18-21.[54] It is probable that *what* is being learned will be significant in any assessment of whether an individual finds learning more difficult at 40 than at 18.

In fact, the amount of psychological and other research which allows for clear-cut conclusions on these questions is limited. The difficulties in conducting longitudinal studies and in isolating independent variables are considerable. Adults may be shown to perform less well on intelligence tests than adolescents but such differential performance is open to a variety of interpretations. Entwistle summarizes that:

> conclusions from the more recent longitudinal and cohort sequential studies show that although there is some decline in intellectual abilities, it does not become marked until old age.[55]

Adults do less well in tests involving rapid solving of certain kinds of problems, in assimilating new information with their existing stocks of knowledge and in retrieving information from memory.[56] Older (pensioner) adults have been shown as consistently less able than younger adults simultaneously to assimilate data and to draw inferences from it.[57] It may not be inappropriate to use the metaphor of a library with ever increasing files of information but with less than up-to-date mechanisms of information retrieval to summarize what the research literature tells us about the effect of ageing on learning among adults.

However, higher education is not exclusively or primarily concerned with the acquisition of information, with the memorization of detail or with the rapid and simultaneous transposition of data into problem solution. Exercise of judgement and of critical, analytical and independent thought flowing from commitment to an intellectual framework are the processes and qualities which most teachers in higher education identify as the objectives of their courses.[58] There is no reason to suppose that adults are not as likely to display these qualities as 18-year-olds, and some would argue that they are more likely to do so either because of their 'maturity' (transmitted through experience of 'the real world' or manifested from absence of the distractions to which young students are prone)[59] or because of the probability that an adult student has an 'intrinsic/intellectual' rather than an 'extrinsic/instrumental' orientation to study.[60] It is, therefore, difficult to advance strong claims that adult students in higher education need different learning and teaching methods from other students on grounds of the effect on ageing on learning ability. However, Entwistle rightly argues that for adult students:

> particular attention will have to be paid to locating and remedying incomplete understanding of the 'anchoring ideas' and basic interpretative or analytic skills of the discipline.... It will also be important to provide 'ideational scaffolding' to help the students organize their developing knowledge effectively, and ensure that they are not overburdened initially either with unnecessary factual detail or with excessive workloads.[61]

It is more probable that, because of the variety of adult matriculation routes into higher education, adult students will be less likely to have acquired this ideational scaffolding than younger students and will be slower to construct it for themselves.

Hopper and Osborn describe the adult student in higher education as having entered a 'marginal situation', involving 'cross pressures, resocialisation and isolation', particularly if entering a full-time course.[62] To some extent the marginality is real in the sense that adult students in degree courses are a minority and their domestic, social and perhaps, financial situation is likely to be different from that of the majority of their peers. To a more important extent the marginality is a social construct, deriving from the role of higher education institutions in the initial education of the young.

The research literature[63] and what may be termed the 'second chance' literature[64] agree that adult students in higher education normally initially lack self-confidence in relation to their studies and harbour considerable fear of failure. Again, such factors must be subject to individual differences of personality and temperament but such feelings for adult students are to a degree rational and situational. They have made bigger leaps into the unknown than the younger students who have progressed directly from school; they do not have the advantage (although some higher education teachers regard it as a disadvantage) of two or three years full-time sixth-form work with steady knowledge acquisition and routine practice at note taking, assignments and examinations, and some will have much more at stake than the 18-year-olds – they have sacrificed paid work and taken a reduction in income for their families and themselves.

The paradox is that, in the perception of those who teach them, adult students in higher education appear to be more confident than younger students. In part, social confidence is confused with academic confidence; in part, a greater community of interest may appear to be present between middle-aged students and middle-aged lecturers. Anecdotal and research evidence record that adult students ask more questions, talk more in seminars, remain more clearly in lecturers' memories, etc.[65] Indeed, lecturers may depend on the adult student's contribution to keep a sagging discussion buoyant and group pressures may define for the adult student the role of discussion leader.

Claims that courses in higher education should be different because all or a majority of students upon them are adult run immediately into epistemological deep water. Such claims normally take the form of one or more of the following:

a   Adults do not have the detailed stock of knowledge accumulated by younger students over seven years of secondary education and therefore *either*:
  i   higher education should provide that detailed knowledge;
      *or*
  ii  course objectives should not require the possession of the detailed knowledge.
b   Adults have knowledge ('commonsense knowledge') and experience ('life experience') which should be utilized (indeed given credit for) in higher education courses.
c   Adults should be treated as such and not be presented with pre-determined curricula but allowed to negotiate content appropriate to their learning objectives.

Talk about courses in institutions of higher education, of course, normally uses a vocabulary including words such as 'advanced', 'academic', 'theory', 'research-based', 'critical' and 'analysis', and it is therefore both philosophically and politically difficult to assert (no matter what happens in practice sometimes) that courses in which there are adults should replicate school education or deal with elementary stages of a discipline. Empirically, there is little evidence that adults wish to have different curricula from other students and a strong impression that they would fear for the credibility of their degrees if they did. Similarly, there is little evidence that adults, any more than other students, wish to negotiate their course content, although in the small number of independent study schemes in higher education adults have been proportionately over-represented. It seems that such schemes have had a valuable function for students, whether adult or not, who have been dissatisfied with conventional teaching and divergent and confident enough to design their own studies.[66]

Nor is there particularly strong evidence that adults wish their 'life experience' to be utilized in their studies or that pedagogically or philosophically satisfactory ways have been found of doing so. Necessarily, at a certain level, the theory of a discipline will be better understood and retained if it is used by the student to explain or to organize personal experience. Conversely, tutors sometimes comment on the need to divert older students from over-emphasis on anecdotal experience as a substitute for objective evidence to prove a point. Nevertheless, the utilization and accreditation of experience in higher education is identified in current conventional wisdom as an important subject of further clarification. The UGC Working Party on Continuing Education recommended that 'universities ... develop procedures for assessing learning by experience as a way for mature students to satisfy admissions requirements.'[67] Evans, rather more boldly, urges that 'academic institutions need to be prepared to accept learning from ... all kinds of sources ... on the same terms as learning derived from their own formally provided course, if it meets acceptable criteria, and they are asked to do so.'[68]

## Conclusion

In arguing that society must 'recognise adults as learners' and in exploring the implications of what he means, Evans begins from a vision of society as it might be rather than from an analysis of what is pragmatically possible in the short term.

This chapter has given considerable support, where possible drawn from evidence, to Evans' general argument that adults as learners are incidental to institutions of higher education. They are present in universities and in advanced further education in considerable numbers, but (apart, perhaps, from the provision of extra-mural departments) their presence is an historical accident and provision for them is neither nationally uniform nor equitable. But in the present situation of political and economic restraint in British higher education, it is not rational to expect a dramatic reversal of the situation or to require institutions of higher education in the short term to place the adult learner at the centre of their concerns – however desirable that might be.

What we can hope to do is to formulate the professional and experimental approach to provision for adult learners, informed by a connected value framework, which was mentioned above. We can seek to understand more about the effects of ageing on learning in different subject areas and to substitute knowledge about the pedagogic and curriculum structures appropriate for the variety of adults for the myth and rhetoric that currently exists. We must look for a higher education system in which there are fewer extraordinary differences between institutions in provision for adult learners and in which adult learners are represented in fairer proportions according to age, sex, social class and minority group membership. But, above all, as this chapter comes to argue, to do so implies making it possible for adult learners to make use of the educational facilities and expertise of institutions of higher education in ways other than as degree students. It does not require significant resource to open academic institutions in a variety of ways to adult learners. It does require institutional will and commitment to innovate.

# Notes and References

1   Advisory Council for Adult and Continuing Education (1979) *Towards Continuing Education: A Discussion Paper* Leicester, p. 21
2   Woodley, A. (1981) Age bias. In Warren Piper, D. (Ed) *Is Higher Education Fair?* Guildford: SRHE, pp. 80-103
3   Wynne, R. (1979) *The Adult Student and British Higher Education* Amsterdam: European Cultural Foundation, pp. 6-7
4   Woodley *op. cit.*, pp. 82-3
5   Calculated from *Statistics of Education, Volume 6, Universities, 1978-9*
6   Jones, H. A. and Williams, K. E. (1979) *Adult Students and Higher Education* Leicester Advisory Council for Adult and Continuing Education
7   Roderick, G. et al. (1981) *Mature Students: A Study in Sheffield* Sheffield: University of Sheffield Division of Continuing Education, p. 52
8   Personal communication from Open University
9   University Grants Committee (1984) *Report of the Continuing Education Working Party* p. 21
10  *ibid.*
11  UGC *University Statistics 1983/84* Volume 1
12  DES (1980) *Continuing Education: Post Experience Vocational Provision for those in Employment: A Paper for Discussion*
13  Whitburn, J., Mealing, M. and Cox, C. (1976) *People in Polytechnics* London: Society for Research into Higher Education
14  Jones and Williams *op. cit.*, p. 18
15  Midwinter, E. (1982) *Age is Opportunity: Education and Older People* London: Centre for Policy on Ageing, p. 25
16  Cutress, N., Morrison, V. and Palmer, F. (1983) The older Open University student *Teaching at a Distance* 24, 28-34
17  Research project on Mature Student Participation in Education (1984) *Final Report to the Department of Education and Science* unpublished, p. 253
18  National Institute of Adult Education (1970) *Adult Education – Adequacy of Provision* London: NIAE, p. 126
19  Percy, K. A. and Powell, J. (1980) A first evaluation of the Open College. In Percy, K. A. and Lucas, S. M. (Eds) *The Open College and Alternatives* Lancaster, pp. 13-14
20  Percy, K. A. (1981) *Report on the 'Open Lectures' Scheme for the Session 1980-1* University of Lancaster, unpublished
21  Wynne *op. cit.*, pp. 14-15
22  *ibid.*, p. 15
23  Tight, M. (1982) *Part-time Degree Level Study in the United Kingdom* ACACE, p. 169
24  Embling, J. (1974) *A Fresh Look at Higher Education: European Implications of the Carnegie Commission Reports* Amsterdam: Elsevier
25  Williamson, B. (1981) Class bias. In Warren Piper, D. (Ed.) *Is Higher Education Fair?* Guildford: SRHE, p. 26
26  Whitburn, Mealing and Cox *op. cit.* summarized in Williamson, B. *op. cit.*, p. 28
27  Charnley, A., Osborn, M. and Withnall, A. (1980) *Review of Existing Research in Adult and Continuing Education, Volume 1, Mature Students*

Leicester: National Institute of Adult Education, para. 3.4a

28 Hopper, E. and Osborn, M. (1975) *Adult Students Education, Selection and Social Control* London: Frances Pinter

29 Percy and Powell *op. cit.*, p. 14

30 McIntosh, N., Calder, J. and Swift, B. (1976) *A Degree of Difference* London: SRHE

31 Roderick et al. *op. cit.*, p. 59

32 McIntosh, Calder and Swift *op. cit.*

33 Charnley, Osborn and Withnall *op. cit.*, p. 43

34 Lucas, S. and Ward, P. (Eds) (1985) *A Survey of 'Access' Courses in England* Lancaster: University of Lancaster School of Education, p. 126

35 Little, A. and Robbins, D. (1981) Race bias. In Warren Piper, D. (Ed.) *Is Higher Education Fair?* Guildford: SRHE, p. 60

36 Advisory Council for Adult and Continuing Education (1982) *Adults: Their Educational Experience and Needs* Leicester, p. 66

37 Tight *op. cit.*, p. 61

38 Woodley, A. and McIntosh, N. E. (1974) *People who decide not to apply to the Open University: An Enquiry into their Reasons and Social Characteristics* Open University, unpublished. Woodley, A. (1978) *Applicants who Decline the Offer to a Place at the Open University: A Preliminary Report* Open University, unpublished

39 Percy and Powell *op. cit.*, pp. 22-23. Percy, K. A., Powell, J. and Flude, C. (1983) *Students in the Open College of the North West: A Follow-up Study* Blagdon: Coombe Lodge, pp. 536-7

40 Advisory Council for Adult and Continuing Education *op. cit.*, p. 106

41 cf Wilson, P.S. (1971) *Interest and Discipline in Education* London: Routledge

42 Woodley *op. cit.*, p. 90

43 Wynne *op. cit.*, pp. 17-23

44 *ibid.*, p. 20

45 Lucas and Ward *op. cit.*

46 Toyne, M., University of Exeter, conducted the investigation in 1977-80 which led to the establishment of ECCTIS

47 Educational Counselling and Credit Transfer Information Service

48 Lovett, T. (1975) *Adult Education, Community Development and the Working Class* Ward Lock

49 Fordham, P., Poulton, G. and Randle, L. (1979) *Learning Networks in Adult Education* London: Routledge

50 Midwinter, E. (Ed.) (1984) *Mutual Aid Universities* London: Croom Helm

51 Neave, G. (1976) *Patterns of Equality* Windsor: National Foundation for Educational Research

52 See, for example, Percy, Powell and Flude *op. cit.*, and Roderick et al. *op. cit.*

53 Woodley *op. cit.*, p. 95

54 Entwistle, N. J. and Wilson, J. D. (1977) *Degrees of Excellence: The Academic Achievement Game* Hodder and Stoughton

55 Entwistle, N. J. (1983) Learning and teaching in universities: the challenge of the part-time adult student. In University of London Goldsmiths' College *Part-time First Degrees in Universities* Conference Report, 8 March. London: Goldsmiths' College, p. 26

56  Thompson, D. (1982) Adult development. In Mitzel, H.E. (Ed.) *Encyclopedia of Educational Research* (5th Edition) London: Collier Macmillan

57  cf Abrams, A. (1982) *Education and Elderly People* London: Age Concern Research Unit, pp. 5-6

58  Percy, K. A. and Entwistle, N. J. (1974) Critical thinking or conformity. In Flood Page, C. and Gibson, J. (1974) *Papers presented at the Ninth Conference of the Society for Research into Higher Education* London: SRHE, pp. 1-30

59  cf Percy and Powell *op. cit.*

60  cf Entwistle *op. cit.*, p. 23

61  *ibid.*, p. 32

62  Hopper and Osborn *op. cit.*

63  eg Roderick et al. *op. cit.*; Percy and Powell *op. cit.*

64  eg Bell, J. and Roderick, G. (1982) *Never too Late to Learn* London: Longman. Rogers, J.(1977) *Adults Learning* Milton Keynes: Open University Press

65  eg Roderick et al. *op. cit.*, pp. 76-7

66  Percy, K. A. and Ramsden, P. (1980) *Independent Study in English Higher Education* London: SRHE

67  University Grants Committee *op. cit.*, p. 41

68  Evans, N. (1985) *Post-Education Society: Recognising Adults as Learners* London: Croom Helm

# 5

# New Technologies

*Kitty Chisholm*

## The Context

A common definition of information technology as 'the acquisition, transmission, processing and presentation of information in all its forms', being broad enough to include the whiteboard and the letterpress printing press, emphasizes the need for a working definition for the purposes of this chapter. What most people now understand by IT is the *new* information technologies, based on telecommunications, microelectronics or more particularly, the digital microelectronic circuit. So IT, for the next few pages at least, is shorthand for 'the acquisition, (storage), transmission, processing and presentation of information', using microelectronic and telecommunications technology.

Since IT82, the Government's £2.6m awareness campaign, IT has become a familiar term for a significant proportion of the British public (62% of adults had heard of information technology by the end of the campaign). In many cases the technology (as opposed to the terminology) will have been introduced via the television – via teletext or viewdata – and/or through personal microcomputers (an estimated 12% of British households now own one). The DTI's £16m Micros in Schools project has also had an impact in raising awareness – with some 100,000 micros installed in British schools.

But by 1984 the 'new golden age' messages of such campaigns were swamped by loud demands for more IT education and training and more IT graduates and technicians, from government and industry alike. The publication of the first report of the Butcher Committee gave coherent voice to the demand, and began to put some figures together.[1] Estimates vary, but the shortfall in new graduates in IT in 1984 was assessed by the Alvey Directorate at about 1,500, with some 5,000 more required by 1987/8. The Policy Studies Institute's estimated shortfall of 21,000 for engineers with microelectronics expertise, also quoted by Butcher, is significantly higher, and positively frightening when compared to the total student numbers in engineering and technology in higher education (universities, including the OU, and advanced HE) of 66.6 thousand in 1981-2.[2]

The message from Butcher is clearly that, in spite of current mechanisms to increase output in the IT related subjects, such as 'new blood' posts for universities, the DES' IT in Higher Education postgraduate conversion courses, the MSC's TOPS upgrading courses and companies' own training programmes helped by the MSC and the DTI, a massive additional educational and training effort will be necessary if Britain is to have the skills necessary to keep up with international competition.

It is also clear that, if this effort is to have significant effect before 1988, continuing education must play a major role by providing conversion, updating and upgrading courses which are specialized, flexible and easy to access. The role of distance teaching in such provision is particularly mentioned by Butcher.

In addition to this perhaps short-term role, continuing education has a longer-term role in the provision of IT courses, one so obvious that it is not often spelled out, the continuing requirement for keeping skills and knowledge up to date. The newly appointed engineer of 1985, as well as the new graduate, will need updating in four or five years' time. Microelectronic-based technology is developing so rapidly that new discipline areas are even now being evolved to cope with the new skills required – software engineering is one example. Whereas the whole of the higher education sector is being mobilized to respond to the IT skills shortages, it is the continuing education sector which must sustain and underpin that growth, and ensure that the education and training provided is both efficient and cost-effective in the long term.

In spite of the significant increase in the numbers of engineering and technology students on full-time, part-time and sandwich courses in higher education (27% between 77/78 and 81/82, when total numbers increased by 13%), current provision is not meeting demand – and the responses to the demand seem unimaginative expansions of traditional facilities. Even the two new 'IT Universities' put forward in 1984 as rival candidates for joint government and industrial funding were cast in a familiar mode: bringing students to one site for one or two-year face-to-face conversion courses.

In spite of the excitement and glamour of IT, particularly in its recent ability to attract research funding, it would seem that IT-related subjects are on the whole taught mainly through face-to-face courses, with more or less emphasis on hands-on or workshop experience in conventional buildings, at least at undergraduate and graduate level.

# Industrial Training

In spite of the potential of IT for extending access to education (eg through satellite and cable transmission), it would seem that the higher education sector has been slow to implement, as part of its course provision, the tools and systems with which it is becoming familiar for research. A recent study commissioned by the EEC shows the higher education sector lagging behind industrial training in the application of IT, with a few notable exceptions, mainly in continuing education.[3]

Industry uses IT for training for a number of reasons. Computer based training (CBT) can be an efficient way to train people to use computers and other sophisticated equipment; it can affect motivation positively when used for skills training in microelectronic-based systems; it can be cost-effective if used to train large numbers at their own places of work, which may be spread around more than one country. Industry is also beginning to use distance teaching methods, some based on IT delivery systems.

The MSC is supporting and encouraging this trend, and in some cases funding innovative development work in the newest of new technologies, such as artificial intelligence and interactive videodisc. The Training Technologies Division is increasing its development activity to reach not only industrial and commercial training but also the 'training of trainers' in IT skills for the Youth Training Scheme and non-advanced further education. MSC funding for new training technologies is not trivial (one major commercial embedded CBT project is costing some £750k) and reflects the importance placed in using IT to train, as well as in training in IT skills.

## Using IT to teach

But what can IT do for education, as opposed to training? It is most difficult, even for an enthusiast, to be convincing about the educational potential of IT through written accounts alone. Hands-on experience of a number of varied applications is needed if educators are to appreciate what IT has to offer – and why, in many cases, that offer has not been taken up. Just to give some idea of the range of possible educational applications, the following list is quoted:

a  teaching about computers
b  using applications packages
c  continuous assessment
d  electronics blackboard
e  database access
f  electronic mail and telesoftware
g  tutorial CAL systems
h  problem-solving monitors
i  drill and practice systems
j  simulations
k  modelling
l  learning management[4]

'Old' IT is what those in higher education are already using: text, audiotape, telephone, TV, videotape. Educators are accustomed to judging the relative merits of such tools, are familiar with potential operational problems (fuses blown, 'noisy' telephone line) and are confident in handling most of them some of the time. The addition of a computer, or microprocessor, which allows these media to be capable of being transformed into teaching tools of some considerable power, 'still needs some getting used to.' Many see this additional power only in terms of quantity – more information being made available to more people – or in terms of threats to teaching jobs, or to teacher control of learning. In order to see the new IT as an extension of the tools already available, perhaps only a single common thread need be mentioned, affecting the whiteboard-based lesson just as much as the CAL one, that of 'rubbish in – rubbish out.'

However, unless educators are given more opportunities to experiment with IT in their own teaching it will remain most difficult to evaluate its potential. There is, as yet, almost no evidence for the educational effectiveness of computer aided learning (CAL) compared to more conventional methods, and little hard evidence for its cost-effectiveness. The development of good educational software is the major element of the considerable upfront investment that CAL requires, and again there is not sufficient software development at higher education level to be able to compare costs effectively with more traditional methods. One reason for the lack of educational software is that markets are limited because of lack of standardization: versioning software for a number of operating systems is expensive and time-consuming.

IT based teaching is by no means an easy solution to all current problems in higher education. It is, however, a potential solution to some of them – particularly those concerned with large numbers of students and geographical spread. It is also an obvious solution to the problems of teaching about IT, which combines the need to reach large numbers of students and the need for frequent updating.

Using IT to teach IT is sound teaching practice (learning by doing), but IT can be – and has been – used to teach a very broad range of subjects: chemistry, statistics, biology, German, materials science, law, educational psychology, physics, management skills – and so on. One detailed example, of an interactive videodisc used for revision in a materials science course, may help to illustrate some of the teaching methodologies involved, and some of the limitations, in one IT-based system.

## The Teddy Bears Disc

The Teddy Bears disc was developed for an Open University second level course on the structure of materials, T252 *Introduction to Engineering Materials*. Since 1981 the course had offered, as part of the summer school, a series of computer aided learning tutorials which had proved popular with students. The aim of the disc was to offer distance-taught students a concentrated opportunity to revise the concepts presented in the course by applying them to a real-life problem. The disc was based on an existing TV programme, a reconstruction of a court case assessing responsibility for failure of a batch of Teddy Bears' eyes. The existence of the programme enabled the production team to concentrate on the teaching system, rather than the presentation of content. The disc was used by a total of forty students in their free time during the T252 July 1984 summer school. The evaluation was based on observation, recording of interaction, interviews and questionnaires.

For the purpose of this revision, students assumed the role of technical expert, required to conduct experiments, interpret the results, and present the evidence: 'The barristers set up the problem at the beginning of the trial; the video stops and the computer gives the student the opportunity to predict possible causes of eye-loss by the teddy bears, guiding them towards the concept of "environmental stress"; returning to the trial, this point is reinforced as the prosecution makes the case that the cause could have been environmental stress, but the defence counters by claiming that the changes made in the washers were irrelevant to this; back to the computer-controlled simulation of experiments to check the validity of this claim, using some video still-frames; and so on....' Thus the student experiences a continual alternation between video sequences lasting four to five minutes, and computer-controlled exercises lasting ten to fifteen minutes.[5]

The software design was based on STAF2 (Butcher 1982), the latest version of the STAF authoring language developed by the CALCHEM project of the UK National Development programme in Computer Assisted Learning. STAF2 was designed and developed under the co-ordination of the OU Academic Computing Service, and has been widely used for supporting tutorial CAL systems, at the OU; STAF2 is also used as the basis for the OU's Computer Feedback and Assessment System for 'level 3' feedback – ie personalized response letters offering detailed remedial help as well as feedback on performance levels.

This authoring language allows for open-ended questions, and sophisticated answer-matching algorithms which ensure that the system's response to a learner's input is meaningful: eg never accepting a wrong answer as a right one, and accepting more than one level of right answer, according to the importance placed on the question by the development team.

Although in some ways the use of an existing TV programme was a positive factor – not least in cutting down time and cost – it had one major disadvantage, its essentially linear character. Originally not even intended for use as a video, but as broadcast TV, its strong narrative line, essential for broadcast, imposed its own structure on the 'lesson'. Following initial tests, the team adapted the design of the software so as to give learners more information and hence more control. At any point on the disc the learner now can:

a call up detailed contents lists (up to 15) to find out what options are available;
b find out where he/she is in relation to the 'lesson' as a whole;
c choose the next action from a number of options.

In addition, at the beginning of each section, the learners are given an estimate of how long that section will take.

Nine different forms of interaction were designed into the Teddy Bears disc:

1 *Information testing* Straightforward questions of fact, testing knowledge (eg which class of polymers fail in a brittle way).
2 *Information giving* Factual information provided as feedback to questions, often serving as remedial tuition.
3 *Tested observation* Questions designed to test the learner's understanding and interpretation of data, presented in pictorial form, often including some guidance as to how to interpret the data.
4 *Untested observation* The direction of learners' attention to particular details (eg look at the end-on views of fracture surfaces), but without follow-up questioning, or directions as to how to use the observation.
5 *Hypothesis framing* Questions requiring the learner to use knowledge acquired from the disc as well as from previous reading to answer real problems (eg what was the cause of the eye failure), particularly useful in showing the learner how theory links with practice.
6 *Procedure information* Used as feedback to help learners find answers

(eg ultimate tensile strength can be read off the vertical axis).
7 *Hints* Suggestions designed to guide students towards relevent information.
8 *Instructions* Straightforward directives, often remedial in form (eg be more precise, try again).
9 *Simulation* Allowing students to perform surrogate experiments.

The OU students who used the disc for revision at their summer school spent on average one minute per interaction. On the whole, they found this way of learning interesting and stimulating enough to spend a long time working through the disc – an average of 2.25 hours, often longer than they had intended. Students felt that this method of working made them think and question their own knowledge, and the analysis of their interactions for the evaluation report confirmed this perception.

Following the testing of the disc in July 1984, and the further refinement of the system to give learners a greater measure of control, the Teddy Bears disc was submitted for the Philips interactive videodisc awards, and won a gold medal.

It is important to realize that this disc was developed as an experiment, and that not one member of the team was ever working full-time on its development. The quality of the final system reflects the team's emphasis on educational objectives and strategies, on the constant refinement of the software, and on the sophistication of its answer-matching algorithms; in other words the technology was made to serve educational objectives.

## Value to the Individual Learner

The examples of IT applications given above will have shown that their advantages are more apparent for the individual learner. The learner who has a more active role, receives rapid, personalized feedback and has control of pace, process, level and medium is not only more independent, but more committed and interested. Although IT can be used as a 'gimmick' to attract and hold attention, the emphasis on learner involvement and control in most IT-based teaching makes such applications ideal for the adult mature learner looking to continuing education to meet specific objectives.

There are some kinds of learning situations, such as simulations of expensive or dangerous experiments, which, if they are to be cost-effective, can only be offered via IT. Equally, computer modelling of complex processes and systems allows for experiments which in real time might not be possible at all, such as an exercise on improving the financial performance of a company by 1987. There are also subjects which have been totally transformed by computing. Design is one example, where the capability of 'putting your thoughts into 3D' is so valuable that the use of this enabling technology is essential.

## Use of IT in Higher Education

The Teddy Bears' disc is one example which indicates that the technology exists, can be used for educationally sound purposes, and, at least subjectively for the learner, it works. The EEC survey, mentioned above, is a valuable source for other examples of IT in current use in higher education.

Graduate and postgraduate management courses have emerged as some of the most advanced users of IT to teach other than IT-related subjects. Aimed at practising managers, CAL offers not only simulation and modelling of real life problems and processes, but a greater degree of learner independence than conventional courses, and the chance to make mistakes in private!

The 'pioneers' in the use of IT in teaching have been those institutions with close links with industry, and/or strong departments of educational technology, amongst which the OU, with its additional requirements because of its distance teaching role, has experimented most publicly of all.

Factors inhibiting the adoption of IT in the higher education sector are complex and interrelated. Interestingly, cost is often not the first to be mentioned nor the most important for those institutions already using some IT. The lack of well designed educational software, inadequate institutional commitment and 'the conservatism of educators', are more frequently mentioned. The need for adequate training of trainers is also a recurrent theme.

The cost of developing good educational software is very high (on one estimate it can take up to four man months to produce one hour of CAL).[6] Putting teaching into software should be a salutary discipline, like teaching at a distance through text, audio and video. The teacher is forced to set explicit aims and objectives, to think through strategies, to structure lessons clearly, carefully and openly. The need to build in learner interactions forces the teacher to try to question the subject from the learner's point of view. Putting 'chalk and talk' teaching technology onto a computer won't work, just as sending a text book through the post, even with an audio cassette attached, is not distance teaching!

## Using IT to reach

Desktop microcomputers are now more powerful than the 'room full' of computers of the late 50s and early 60s. The increase in power/size has been accompanied by a decrease in cost comparable to being able to buy a Rolls for the price of a box of matches. Use of new telecommunications technology in the USA and Canada – cable and satellite – has enabled access to learning where previously, for reasons of distance or geography, there was none. Both cable and satellite require significant upfront capital investment, however, on a scale needing national rather than institutional investment. If, in the next five to ten years, a micro were to be available in every home in the Uk and significant investment in telecommunications links were a reality, then we might see 'the demise ... of the conventional campus-based higher education institution as we know it.'[7] In other words, all higher education could become continuing education, with learning available 'on tap' at home or at work, to individuals and groups, throughout adult life.

In the meantime, even currently available communications technologies are not being fully exploited for educational purposes in the UK. A number of systems could be used for the delivery of continuing education, not only for the geographically isolated learner, but for those who cannot or will not take a substantial amount of time off work for full- or part-time courses. Sitting at home or in the office a learner could receive study materials, tuition, assessment, counselling and advice, could take part in group tutorials and seminars, could 'attend' lectures and contribute to discussions.

Teletext systems (such as Oracle and Ceefax) could deliver text, graphics and software. The amount of information that teletext can convey is very limited without dedicated channels, and it is a one-way system, so that its most likely applications for education could be information about courses, brief updating items, etc. Viewdata on the other hand allows access, via the telephone system, to information stored on a central computer, and can be used interactively, so it could deliver CAL-based courses as well as serve as an information retrieval system. Prestel is one example of a viewdata system currently in use.

Cable or satellite delivery of TV or video, when used with the telephone system, can also allow for interactive learning; the learner can communicate in real time during a lecture, taking part in question and answer sessions, whether that lecture is taking place at the local college or across the Atlantic. Linking home or work-based microcomputers to a mainframe, also via the telephone system, allows for different kinds of interaction – computer conferencing and electronic mail. With a conferencing system, as well as sending assignments to a tutor and receiving comments in return, learners can communicate with the tutor and each other in real time, or store these communications in the mainframe (like a series of pigeon holes) to be accessed at convenient times.

One advantage of such a system is that all communications are stored, and can form an additional learning resource – a complete record of a seminar, for example, with all questions and answers recorded.

The systems mentioned above share, with the conventional distance teaching media, the disadvantage of no visual communication between participants. Learning to vocalize visual cues and messages takes time, practice and training, particularly for the teacher who has to structure the learning session in a way which encourages, and sometimes even demands, vocalization from learners. When even vocal cues must be written down, typed on a keyboard and sent, there is a correspondingly greater demand to plan ahead, structure and perhaps impose certain rules or guidelines for individual sessions.

The increased potential for interaction, the ability to deliver information on demand at a time and place convenient to the learner, and the ease with which learning material can be kept up to date are some of the advantages which IT-based delivery systems can offer. Once the necessary communications links have been set up, the costs of such systems depend mainly on the costs of course development, which are high and likely to remain so, the cost of equipment to the individual student (microcomputer, teletext TV) and the cost of transmission. With decreasing equipment costs, the sheer numbers of students who could be taught at a distance begin to make such investment a practical proposition.

Not all IT-based systems require heavy upfront investment. One example of a system using the public telephone may serve to show what is currently possible.

# Cyclops – an OU Experiment in Teleconferencing

Cyclops is a system based on standard, easily available and low-cost equipment: a TV set, stereo audio cassette player, two telephones (one for voice communication and the other for graphics transmission), a light pen, and the Cyclops terminal – a medium resolution graphics terminal. This system was located in eighteen local study centres and used over a period of three years to tutor some 600 students on thirty courses in one OU region – the East Midlands. Using normal telephone conference facilities, up to nine study centres could be linked for a tutorial.

The system is truly interactive, in that all participants can draw, write or change material on the screen with the same display seen by all, as well as share voice communication via the loudspeaking unit (hence the system is called 'shared screen audio graphics or teleconferencing').

In addition to material which was drawn on the screen during the sessions (using a light pen or scribble pad) to explain or illustrate particular teaching points (eg diagrams, graphics, mathematical equations), more complex graphics were prepared beforehand using a special studio where tutors (with no knowledge of computing) could even compile large databases of pictorial material, which could be played back at varying speeds, as linear sequences or stills. Tutors could prepare a diagram of a complex system in such a way as to reveal it bit by bit, ask each student to 'progress' a part of the diagram, and reveal, at the end of the exercise, their own final version – which could of course be corrected by any student!

Teaching via Cyclops requires a great deal of preparation and structuring, as well as 'good management.' Evaluation of the project showed that students found the clarification afforded by the graphics facility most helpful, and the ability to interact was an incentive for increased involvement. In spite of the increased planning and preparatory work, tutors found the system easy to use, and, particularly for visually oriented subjects (biology, geography and technology, for example), a very powerful teaching tool. Some training was given to the OU tutors involved in the experiment, and opportunities provided to share experiences with colleagues.

Using Cyclops for group tutorials is an effective way of delivering tuition to a large number of students at a distance, but it still involves travel to local centres. It leaves the tutor firmly in control of content, pace and structure, although allowing for a certain amount of student choice. It is also possible to use Cyclops as a self-instructional system, where the tutor's commentary is recorded on one track of an audio cassette (which is also used for graphics), for use by an individual student.

Since the early days of the OU experiment, the Cyclops terminal has been reduced to a chip, which can be added to a conventional microcomputer for approximately £50. Further developments in telecommunications are likely to reduce the costs of such systems considerably, so that participants might not need to travel to local centres.

Cyclops has remained an experiment, for the OU, in education, but is being used to train engineers in British Telecom.

# The Impact of IT on Continuing Education

The technology exists. This is not to say that any one IT-based system is the way to teach, but that a range of options are available now, to those who wish to teach a large number of students not only for an intensive 3 or 5 or n-year period, but for a lifelong period of learning. It is now possible for institutions of higher education to become learning brokers, bringing together the most appropriate teacher, medium and learning environment at a time and place which is suited to the individual learner, and at the same time guaranteeing that each learner will share the same standards and quality.

The technology is not being used. The impact on continuing education of the new information technology is still at the level of awareness and experimentation, rather than planning or implementation.

There are three major issues which the higher education sector must address if IT can a) begin to become part of the solution to the problem of more education for IT skills and b) begin to meet the new educational needs imposed throughout adult life by the pace of technological change.

The first issue is that of judgement of the cost-effectiveness of IT-based systems, which must not take place abstracted from the context of educational effectiveness. Installing a new system, where cost-effectiveness is not proven, is a daunting risk for any institution. There is not enough evidence yet on which to begin to base such judgement. In many cases, there seems to be a lack of institutional will to acquire such evidence.

The second issue is that of training the trainers. Unless those who teach in higher education are themselves trained in the use of new information technologies, the traditional, more familiar methods will be used, whether they are suited to a subject or not. If new IT systems are introduced without adequate provision for training, they will not be properly used, and both teachers and learners will not be able to make informed judgements about which system or method would best suit any particular educational needs.

The third issue is that of the availability of high quality educational software. Unless it becomes easy for the non-expert to acquire and use high quality educational software, the hardware will gather dust. Unless software is developed by those who really know how to teach as well as how to program, it will be system rather than learner-oriented, and will not serve to teach anyone anything very much.

Where the cost-effectiveness of IT can be demonstrated implementation often follows. The widespread use of microcomputers for administration in many universities and colleges has given the higher education sector first-hand experience of some of the benefits of IT. It is true to say that the Open University, at least, could not offer such a flexible range of provision to some 100,000 students and clients in the UK without using computers for student records, planning, registration, financial administration, assessment, labelling allocations to tutors, study centres and exam centres, project control, etc.

If the use of the new IT to reach and to teach is to change higher education provision in the UK drastically, it will be because it is the most effective way of providing a continuation of educational provision through-out adult life, not only for skills in IT-related subjects but for many others – from architecture to zoology. It will also be because there is a growing demand for such a continuation of provision, from industry, government and the individual learner.

## References

1 Butcher J. (1984) *The Human Factor: the Supply Side Problem* First Report, IT Skills Shortages Committee, Chairman J. Butcher MP, August
2 Institute of Manpower Studies (1984) *Competence and Competition: Training and Education in the Federal Republic of Germany, the United States and Japan* A report prepared by the Institute of Manpower Studies for the National Economic Council and the Manpower Services Commission
3 Zorkoczy, P. et al. (1984) *Opportunities for Information Technology-based Advanced Educational Technologies* Final Report for the Commission of European Communities, May
4 Computer Board (1983) *Report of the Working Party on Computer Facilities for Teaching in Universities*
5 Laurillard, D. M. (1984) *Videodisc Evaluation Report, The 'Teddy Bears' Disc* CAL Research Group Technical Report 1. IET, The Open University
6 Bates, A. W. (Ed.)(1984) *The Role of Technology in Distance Education* Croom Helm
7 Bates, A. W. (1984) New technology and its impact on conventional and distance education *Times Higher Education Supplement* 26 October

## Further Reading

*Electronics and Power* (1985) Focus 'The Age of IT'. Editorial, January
Fuller, Robert G. (Ed.)(1983) *Using Interactive Videodiscs in Open University Courses* Open University
Hawkridge, David (1983) *New Information Technology in Education* Croom Helm
Hawkridge, David (1984) *The High Technology Academy* Paper delivered at Lancaster, August. Available from the author at IET, The Open University
IT Steering Group (1984) *IT82 Final Report* March

# 6

# Economic Issues

*Maureen Woodhall*

The last fifteen years have seen frequent calls by educationists in some countries for a radical shift of resources from traditional patterns of education, which concentrate provision and resources on young people, to a system of 'recurrent', 'lifelong' or 'continuing education', which would increase opportunities for adults to participate in formal or non-formal education or training and to combine or alternate periods of education, work and other activities, including the care of children and leisure.

The 1972 Faure Report *Learning to be* advocated 'lifelong education', and in 1973 an OECD report called for 'a comprehensive educational strategy for all post-compulsory or post-basic education, the essential characteristic of which is the distribution of education in a recurring way, ie in alternation with other activities, principally with work, but also with leisure and retirement,' which would lead to 'a continuity in learning through one's entire lifetime'.[1] More recently the Advisory Council for Adult and Continuing Education called for 'a radical shift of emphasis by the whole post-school education system towards the educational needs of adults.'[2]

Such a shift is frequently justified on economic grounds. Advocates argue that it would be both more efficient and more equitable than 'front-end' systems which concentrate most resources on full-time, formal education for the young and initial training for new entrants to the labour market. They suggest that a more flexible pattern of education and training opportunities for adults would result in a more highly skilled and adaptable workforce, able to respond to changing economic conditions and new technologies, that it would allow workers to update and upgrade their skills, preventing technical obsolescence of skills, and it would improve the links between education and work. On grounds of equity, also, it can be argued that a redistribution of opportunities is desirable, in favour of older taxpayers, who contribute to the costs of education but received fewer benefits, in the past, than their younger counterparts today.

In order to promote such a shift, some writers have proposed elaborate new financing mechanisms involving 'individual entitlements' or 'drawing rights',[3] which would guarantee subsidies for a period of post-compulsory education or training for everyone, regardless of age. Faced with the financial implications of such a system, however, economists have argued that the costs would be prohibitive and the benefits questionable. The opportunity costs of education, both to society and the individual, are much greater for an older, experienced worker than for a young person, while the remaining working life is much shorter, which reduces the expected lifetime benefits. Thus, the OECD, in first putting forward the case for recurrent education in 1973, argued that 'a cost-benefit analysis, based on classical economic considerations is bound to turn out to the disfavour of recurrent education', but argued that 'social goals such as equality, participation and benefit to the individual ... may outweigh the higher costs in purely economic terms.'[4] Some economists have gone much further, and bitterly attacked the whole concept of recurrent education as simply the latest 'vogue' or 'bandwagon', which lacks any economic justification. For example, Blaug and Mace argue that 'if the recurrent education movement were to succeed, it would prove to be the most expansionary educational proposal that the world has ever seen. Fortunately, there is very little danger that it will succeed.'[5]

One reason why there is so much disagreement about the relative costs and benefits of shifting the balance of educational resources away from youth and initial training, in favour of adults, is that there are widely different definitions and concepts of recurrent, lifelong or continuing education. In some cases, the proposals involve all forms of education or training for adults, including formal and informal, vocational and general. Some writers suggest that young people should be encouraged to postpone post-secondary education until after they have had some work experience, and that thereafter, 'educational opportunities should be spread out over the individual's life-time.'[6] Others simply argue for more opportunities for adults to pursue higher education, or professional training, either because they missed the chance to pursue their education at an earlier age or because they wish to extend or update their earlier education and training in order to acquire new skills, take a refresher course to keep up with the latest technical developments, or retrain for a new job.

Because some of the literature or the proposals for an extension of recurrent or continuing education is 'at best inspirational and at worst vague',[7] there have been few attempts to analyse the economic implications of proposals to shift resources in favour of adults, and establish a truly recurrent or lifelong system of education and most of the existing studies tend to be rather critical. Williams (1977), reviewing the literature on the economics of lifelong education, acknowledged that 'judged by orthodox criteria of evaluation, lifelong education based on conventional methods of educational provision is likely to prove very expensive in the use of resources in relation to the benefits obtained.'[8] An early attempt to apply cost-benefit techniques to the concept of recurrent education did, indeed, conclude that the costs would outweigh the benefits.[9] Two later studies by Stoikov[10] pointed out that proposals for recurrent education fall into two categories, with very different economic implications. If the aim is to encourage widespread postponement of higher education, until after young people have acquired some work experience, this will reduce the value of the investment and lead to a loss rather than a gain in human capital. On the other hand, if the aim is to ensure that adults as well as young people have educational opportunities, ranging from 'second chance' options and refresher courses to post-experience vocational training designed to update, enrich and develop previously acquired knowledge and professional skills, then there are strong economic, as well as social and educational arguments in favour of such policies.

Here we are not concerned with ambitious but vague proposals to introduce lifelong or recurrent education in place of conventional front-end systems, which concentrate most general education and initial vocational training on young people. Nor are we concerned with proposals that require many young people to postpone higher education until after they have gained work experience. It is easier to analyse the economic implications of continuing education *after* a period of full-time initial education than to explore the potential costs and benefits of abandoning the concept of initial education in favour of a regular alternation between education and work or other activities. We are further limiting the field by concentrating on continuing education within higher education, rather than attempting to encompass all the formal and non-formal learning opportunities that exist for adults, including evening classes, correspondence courses, on-the-job training and courses offered by colleges, adult education centres and a host of voluntary agencies.

Nevertheless, the scope is still wide. In their reports on continuing education, the UGC and NAB covered such diverse activities as:

a   Degree-level education for full-time mature students
b   Part-time degree and diploma courses
c   Extra-mural courses
d   Post-experience vocational education courses (PEVE)

Here we consider the economic implications of this range of opportunities for adults by examining the costs and the benefits of continuing education in universities, polytechnics and colleges, from the point of view of:

a   The participants
b   Employers
c   The institutions providing continuing education
d   Society as a whole

The question of how the costs and the benefits of continuing education are shared between individuals, employers, institutions and the State is, of course, crucial to the question of how continuing education should be financed. We therefore start by reviewing the evidence on costs and benefits and then turn to the question of how continuing education is currently financed, and how methods and mechanisms for financing continuing education may change in the future.

## The Benefits of Continuing Education

The economic justification for any form of education or training is either that it represents investment in knowledge and skills which will make workers more productive in the future, or that it is valued for the immediate satisfaction and benefit that it brings to participants. While a short, highly specialized course of professional training, designed to bring doctors or engineers into contact with the latest technical developments, clearly falls in the former category, and a course of extra-mural lectures on the history of art, attended by people wishing to enrich their leisure or retirement, can be regarded as pure consumption, in many cases it is less easy to categorize education as consumption or investment. Adults attending courses in higher education have a variety of motives, they are likely to derive immediate pleasure and satisfaction from learning as well as developing new skills which may or may not help them in their present or future jobs.

Changes in patterns of working life, leading to increased leisure and early retirement are likely to lead to increased demand for continuing education opportunities for reasons of personal development, interest and satisfaction. In some cases this demand may be for occasional lectures or extra-mural courses, but in other cases adults may wish to study for a degree or other qualification, purely for intellectual stimulus or satisfaction.

However, for the majority of adults participation in higher education after the completion of full-time initial education or training is intended to serve some vocational purpose. The aim may be to up-date existing skills or acquire new ones, which will help participants to become more effective in an existing job or to train for a new one. But the report of the NAB Continuing Education Group quotes recent research which 'suggests that most who seek this additional education experience do so with a vocational purpose in mind.'[11]

The economic justifications put forward for vocationally-oriented continuing education for adults include:

a The rapid pace of technological change means that a single 'dose' of initial education and training is insufficient to provide the skills necessary for a whole working lifetime; without constant updating and renewal, technical knowledge and skills will become obsolescent.

b Workers may need to retrain for new jobs to cope with changing labour market conditions, the decline of traditional manufacturing industries and the growth of new occupations and service industries requiring new skills. Continuing education may therefore help to reduce unemployment caused by changes in the demand for traditional skills.

c Continuing education also helps to create an adaptable, flexible workforce, and to overcome skill shortages. Demographic trends mean that the supply of young entrants to the labour force will decline in the late 1980s and 1990s, so that employers will increasingly have to rely on older workers acquiring new skills, and married women returning to the labour force in order to meet new demands.

d Providing continuing education for workers who already have practical work experience means that skills can be learned more quickly and efficiently, and relevant knowledge and skills identified more readily, since theoretical and practical knowledge will complement each other. Thus, it is argued that continuing education for adults will reduce the often-quoted 'mis-match' between the demands of employers and the offerings of the education system.

All these represent direct benefits both to the individual who undertakes continuing education and to employers and the economy at large. The benefits to the individual can be measured in terms of higher lifetime earnings and increased probability of finding employment; those to employers can be measured in terms of higher levels of output, which in turn will lead to higher levels of national income and economic growth, and lower employment.

In addition to these direct benefits, however, it is often suggested that continuing education for adults may bring indirect benefits to the institutions providing continuing education, and that such 'spill-over' benefits will ultimately benefit all participants of higher education, and society as a whole. For example, the UGC Working Party on Continuing Education lists a number of indirect benefits to universities themselves:

a   Relationships with the wider community will be improved by the recognition that universities are an important source of relevant continuing education for society at large.
b   Continuing education will broaden the perspectives of academic staff and bring them into close contact with the needs of industry and society generally, which will mean that new lines of research and consultancy may be identified, new sources of funding tapped and the ability of universities to give practical advice on national and industrial problems enhanced.
c   The knowledge and experience gained by university teachers from their continuing education activities will feed back into regular undergraduate and postgraduate teaching.

In short, economists have discussed, and identified, various economic benefits of continuing education for adults, which take the form of increased productivity, both of participants and of the staff and institutions offering continuing education opportunities. However, there have been virtually no attempts to calculate the monetary value of these benefits. Thus, it is often argued that increased investment in continuing education would lead to a more efficient use of resources in the education sector and in industry, but there are no actual estimates of the returns to such investments.

In addition to these efficiency gains, it is often claimed that there will be equity gains from providing continuing education opportunities, which will widen access to higher education and reduce disparities between social classes and between generations. However, evidence suggests that participants in continuing education are most likely to be those who already have formal education qualifications, and even 'second-chance' opportunities, such as the Open University, frequently benefit those who already have higher than average levels of education. Thus, the redistributive role of continuing education is sometimes questioned, not only in this country but elsewhere. For example, a recent American study concluded that 'Today's adult learners are disproportionately young, white, well educated and earning salaries above the national median family income.'[12]

To sum up, the literature is full of claims of the economic benefits offered by continuing education, but economists have, for the most part, confined their empirical studies of the returns on educational investment to traditional education for the young, or industrial training. There have been studies of the returns on retraining for unemployed workers, but very little hard evidence exists on the magnitude of the economic benefits of continuing education in higher education.

## The Costs of Continuing Education

The opportunity costs of higher education, in the form of income foregone, are much higher for adults than for young people. Even if they lack formal education, their work experience means that the average earnings of adult workers are higher than the foregone earnings of those who enter higher education straight after school. The opportunity cost of full-time higher education for adults is therefore substantial, which is why economists, such as Stoikov, have been sceptical of the wisdom of postponing higher education. The opportunity cost of students' time, usually measured in terms of foregone earnings, increases the private cost to the individual, who must sacrifice paid employment in order to undertake continuing education, as well as the social costs, since total production is reduced if an experienced worker leaves employment for full-time education.

On the other hand, if there is unemployment, the opportunity cost to society is reduced. If the alternative to continuing education is not productive work but unemployment, then there is no loss of production (or earnings), and both the private and social costs of retraining an unemployed worker are therefore lower than the costs of continuing education for the employed.

Some economists have therefore argued that government funds that are currently used to finance unemployment benefit could, at no extra cost to society, be more productively used to finance continuing education. Emmerij (1983) estimated that in the Netherlands there are approximately 370,000 unemployed adults who could benefit from recurrent education or retraining, and he proposed that money now allocated to social security payments should be used to finance education and training opportunities, with training allowances for the unemployed. This would represent no greater drain on public funds than the present system of unemployment benefit: 'Instead of spending for *negative* reasons ... the same amount of money could be used for *positive* reasons.'[13] More recently the NAB Continuing Education Group pointed out that an increase in the number of workers 'released to undergo necessary updating would provide some vacancies in the labour market, and thus contribute to the reduction in unemployment. The net fiscal cost of providing these opportunities is relatively small, when the cost of financial support to the unemployed is taken into account.'[14]

However, although the resource costs of continuing education are lower during periods of unemployment, they are not zero. The direct costs of tuition still have to be met and in some cases the costs of educating mature students may be higher than the costs of education for young people straight from school. Mature students may need additional counselling, if they are unused to formal education; they may expect better facilities or lower student/teacher ratios than younger students. On the other hand, it is often suggested that mature students are more highly motivated and may learn more quickly, which would reduce costs.

Another factor which may reduce the costs of continuing education in higher education at a time of declining birthrate is the existence of spare capacity, due to demographic fluctuations. The size of the traditional age group for higher education will diminish in the next decade, creating spare capacity that could be utilized for continuing education. The marginal cost of providing courses for adults would then be lower than average costs at present, provided that existing facilities or staff could be re-allocated to continuing education.

Continuing education for adults often takes the form of part-time, rather than full-time courses, which reduces both the private and the social opportunity costs, as Wagner (1977) shows in his comparisons of the costs of the Open University and conventional universities.[15] However, for this reason it is often very difficult to obtain realistic estimates of the direct costs of continuing education, since it is notoriously difficult to calculate the costs of part-time courses. Both the UGC and NAB reports on continuing education recognize that current financing mechanisms incorporating weights for converting part-time students to full-time equivalents do not adequately reflect the true resource costs of part-time courses, but very little accurate information is available on true resource costs.

Since 1970, universities have been asked to make an assessment of the full economic costs of post-experience vocational education courses, distinguishing between:

a  Costs directly attributable to PEVE (eg staff specially recruited and materials used specifically for such courses)

b  Overheads (eg administrative staff time, the use of university buildings, libraries etc.)

Having estimated the full economic cost of PEVE, universities are free to set their fees for such courses higher or lower, although they are expected to cover at least the directly attributable costs. Universities are also free to set their own fees for part-time degree and diploma students, but the UGC considers that most universities have been charging fees that are too low.[16]

Clearly, more accurate estimates of the true costs of continuing education are needed in order to formulate realistic fee policies. NAB argues strongly that any fee policy for part-time and other mature students must be consistently applied across all three sectors currently providing continuing higher education: the universities, the public sector and the Open University. At present, the proportion of costs recovered through fees varies considerably. However, this is simply one aspect of the confusion which currently characterizes the finance of continuing education.

# Finance for Continuing Education in Higher Education

The question of who should pay for continuing education, ie whether the financing burden should fall on the individual, the employer or the taxpayer, depends crucially on the magnitude and the distribution costs and benefits, but as we have seen, it is not easy to answer the question with any precision.

In his classic formulation of the economics of human capital, Becker (1964) made a crucial distinction between *general* education or training, which increases a worker's productivity in a wide range of jobs, and *specific*, work-related training, which increases the worker's productivity only in a single job. He argued that the way education or training is financed depends on whether it is general or specific. Employers will be willing to bear the cost of specific training, since they will reap benefits in the form of higher levels of output from more skilled workers. On the other hand, no single employer will be willing to finance general education or training. The costs of this will fall instead on the individual, who must accept lower wages while receiving training, but subsequently will enjoy financial returns, in the form of higher earnings. However, if general education is believed to offer externalities, the government should also bear some of the costs, by providing subsidies, in order to prevent under-investment.

The question of who will reap the benefits of training is central to the current debate about how the costs of industrial training should be shared between government employers and individuals. The White Paper *Training for Jobs*, and the subsequent changes in methods of financing work-related courses in non-advanced further education, the announcement of a pilot scheme of training loans, and government attempts to persuade employers to increase their spending on vocational training, all reflect the government's intention of shifting some of the financial burden from the taxpayer to employers and individual trainees.

The same issues arise when we consider how the costs of continuing education in higher education should be shared between employers or other sponsors, individuals and public funds. It is clear that continuing education does offer benefits to employers, individuals and society at large. The question is, who should pay for such benefits? The UGC Working Party on Continuing Education looked particularly at post-experience vocational courses, and concluded:

> We acknowledge that PEVE benefits both employers and participants and that they should bear most of the costs. But there are benefits to society above and beyond those to individual employers and participants for which they cannot be expected to foot the bill. We believe that a significant contribution from the public purse is both justified and essential if post-experience vocational education is to develop to meet the nation's needs.

The Working Party concludes that the present 'token contribution' provided through UGC funds of £142 per full-time equivalent student is not sufficient, in view of the costs of designing and marketing courses and the wider benefits of keeping highly trained professionals up to date in their knowledge and skills. The report therefore recommends a subsidy of £500 per FTE student, and urges that this should be 'additional money, not simply a recycling of existing resources.'[17]

Two questions are raised. First, is £500 per student the optimum level of subsidy? This depends partly on the extent of the indirect benefits that are believed to 'spill-over' to other students and to society at large. Secondly, should such subsidies be given to institutions, to enable them to offer courses at lower fees, or alternatively, to individuals to enable them to pay realistic fees. Subsidies to providers may encourage the development of new courses, while subsidies to individuals may encourage responsiveness to the needs of individual students or sponsors.

At present, individuals wishing to undertake continuing education may be financed by their employers through paid educational leave (PEL), or must finance themselves, with or without financial support from their local education authority. A study of PEL[18] estimated that in 1976-7 between three and four million people (15% to 20% of the work force) benefited from PEL, and about 40% of all PEL involved courses in higher or further education. The UK, along with many other countries, ratified the 1974 Resolution of the International Labour Organization (ILO) which called upon countries to promote PEL, but a recent survey of PEL provision in Europe presented a 'fairly gloomy picture'[19] and concluded that in the current economic climate in Europe the scope for significant expansion of PEL is limited, although expansion is desirable on both social and economic grounds. The study quotes the view of the Confederation of British Industry in the UK, that 'the only criterion' which could be applied in deciding whether employees should be released for PEL is 'the needs of the firm in question.'[20] This underlines the point that even if PEL provisions were to be expanded, it would still leave many adults unable to benefit, particularly the unemployed, those outside the labour market, and those wanting to pursue non-vocational courses. Even within the workforce, Killeen and Bird showed that at present PEL is very unevenly distributed between different occupations, with more than 50% of all PEL going to managers, professional, scientific and technical employees.

There are some alternative sources of financial support, including Manpower Services Commission programmes for the unemployed, and the Training Opportunities Scheme (TOPS), as well as general financial support for students in higher education, but it has been frequently emphasized[21] that the present pattern of student support favours the traditional, full-time student entering higher education straight from school, at the expense of mature students and those studying part-time. The mandatory grant system does not extend to part-time students or to those who already have a qualification. Thus, although mature students following a full-time course do receive higher grants than those under 25, many adults taking continuing education courses do not qualify for any financial support.

The government is currently reviewing the whole pattern of student support, in the light of the abortive attempt, in November 1984, to reintroduce fees for upper income students. The results and proposals are not yet available, although they will be announced in the summer of 1985, when we will know whether the government has accepted the many proposals that have been made for a system of student loans.

There are strong grounds for advocating the introduction of loans for some students in higher education, and students following certain types of continuing education are obvious candidates. Loans would enable adults to finance courses which would bring direct financial benefits, and then to repay their loans out of their higher subsequent earnings. The experimental system of training loans, announced by the MSC in 1984, is a small step in this direction, which could well be extended to other forms of continuing education.

It can also be argued that a combined system of loans and grants for all students in higher education would free resources which could be used to provide subsidies for those who currently receive no grant from public funds, including adults taking part-time courses. Thus, advocates of loans argue that a combined loan and grant system could be more flexible and more equitable than the present system of student support, which concentrates financial aid on a small minority.[22]

However, there will always be students for whom loans – even if backed by a government guarantee and offered at subsidized interest rates – would be insufficient. There have been a number of proposals in recent years, for radical new forms of support for adults in continuing education, including individual 'entitlements' or 'drawing rights' which would entitle all adults to a period of subsidized education, to be taken at a time of their choice. It is suggested that such a system could be financed by means of a pay-roll tax, or compulsory contributions to a 'Training Fund' such as exists in Sweden or France. A recent review of actual and proposed methods for financing recurrent education[23] looks at experience in France, Sweden, Germany, the Netherlands and the USA, and examines public, private and 'para-fiscal' financing, which involves both public and private sources of funds, such as the Industrial Training Boards in Britain in the 1970s. However, the authors conclude that no country has yet devised a comprehensive, flexible and efficient system for financing recurrent education and training. The strengths and weaknesses of alternative financing mechanisms have recently been reviewed by Drake (1983), who also recommends no ideal model.[24]

The fact is that any proposals for a system of financing which attempts to cover all forms of continuing education and training for adults are likely to prove vague and impractical. Continuing education serves different needs and must continue to be funded from a variety of sources. What is needed is a combination of sources of funds and financing mechanisms which ensure that the costs are shared equitably between individuals, employers and taxpayers and appropriate incentives are provided for institutions to offer, and for individuals to participate in a variety of courses.

The NAB Continuing Education Group, reviewing the present pattern of finance for continuing education referred to the view, 'which we share, that the emphasis of existing funding arrangements reflects an almost total concern with initial education.' The solution, according to the NAB report, is not a massive injection of new funds, so much as a shift in the balance of funding, in order to give greater priority to part-time and post-experience vocational education. The NAB report cautions against the assumption that 'finance is the panacea for all problems', but argues much more modestly that 'The importance of finance is that when applied at points of most pressure, it can be the most effective lubricant for oiling the wheels of change, while lack of it can sometimes be the most effective brake.'[25]

By examining the principles and criteria by which continuing education is provided and funded through higher education institutions, and suggesting ways in which this provision can become more effective in the future, it may be possible to identify these 'points of pressure', and contribute to the development of a more rational policy for sharing the financial burdens in the future.

# References

1  OECD (1973) *Recurrent Education: A Strategy for Lifelong Learning* Paris: Organization for Economic Co-operation and Development, p.24
2  ACACE (1982) *Continuing Education: From Policies to Practice* Leicester: Advisory Council for Adult and Continuing Education, p.v
3  Levin, H. M. and Schütze, H. G.(Eds) (1983) *Financing Recurrent Education: Strategies for Increasing Employment, Job Opportunities and Productivity* London: Sage
4  OECD *op. cit.*, p.69
5  Blaug, M. and Mace J. (1977) Recurrent education: the New Jerusalem *Higher Education* 6, 277
6  OECD *op. cit.*
7  Blaug, M. (1973) *Education and the Employment Problem in Developing Countries* Geneva: International Labour Office, p.73
8  Williams, G. (1977) *Towards Lifelong Education: A New Role for Higher Education Institutions* Paris: UNESCO, p.109
9  Gannicott, K. (1971) *Recurrent Education: A Preliminary Cost-Benefit Analysis* Paris: OECD
10  Stoikov, V. (1973) Recurrent education: some neglected economic issues *International Labour Review* 108, August-September. Also Stoikov, V. (1975) *The Economics of Recurrent Education and Training* Geneva: International Labour Office
11  National Advisory Body (1984) *Report of the Continuing Education Group* London: NAB
12  Christoffel, P. (1983) An opportunity deferred: lifelong learning in the US. In Levin and Schütze *op. cit.*, p.27
13  Emmerij, L. (1983) Paid educational leave: a proposal based on the Dutch case. In Levin and Schütze *op. cit.* pp. 297-316
14  National Advisory Body *op. cit.*
15  Wagner, L. (1977) The economics of the Open University revisited *Higher Education* 6
16  University Grants Committee (1984) *Report of the Continuing Education Working Party* London: UGC, p.21
17  *ibid.*, p.24
18  Killeen, J. and Bird, M. (1981) *Education and Work: A Study of Paid Educational Leave in England and Wales 1976/7* Leicester: National Institute of Adult Education
19  European Centre for the Development of Vocational Training (1984) *Educational Leave and the Labour Market in Europe* Berlin: CEDEFOP, p.194
20  *ibid.*, p.114
21  ACACE *op. cit.* Also Woodhall, M. (1983) Financial support for students. In Morris, A. and Sizer, J. (Eds) *Resources and Higher Education* Guildford: SRHE, pp. 81-111
22  Woodhall *op. cit.*
23  Levin and Schütze *op. cit.*
24  Drake, K. (1983) *Financing Adult Education and Training* Manchester Monographs No. 21. Manchester: Department of Adult and Higher Education
25  National Advisory Body *op. cit.*, p.42

# 7

# Policy, Obligation and Right

*Michael Richardson*

## Questions of Definition

It may not have gone unnoticed that the Robbins Report[1] which has shaped so much of our present higher education policy context makes no reference to continuing education as such. Its terms of reference related, of course, to full-time higher education. However, in paragraphs 510 to 518 the report did raise flags for 'part-time study and professional education' and 'the education of adults.' It envisaged a continuing growth in part-time study – 'nothing but good' coming from 'a more intimate co-operation between professional bodies and institutions of higher education.' It acknowledged that higher education was 'not a once for all process' and saw that as the pace of discovery quickened it would become increasingly important for practitioners to take courses at intervals to bring them up to date in their subjects. Indeed a 'rapid development of such courses in University institutions' is one of the recommendations made in the body of the report.

Six years later the report of the Planning Committee for the Open University, itself ushering in a new institution which would now be described as an institution of continuing education – also avoided the use of those words as a definition.[2] It spoke of the work of the university in meeting the 'backlog of adults denied and anxious for higher education.' It also identified an important role 'arising from the changes in and the increasing rate of change within modern technological society'. Furthermore, in quoting the Swann Report on the flow into employment of scientists, engineers and technologists, it points out that industry cannot release all the people all of the time to attend updating and refresher courses.[3] It also suggests a very special contribution through the combined services of broadcasting correspondence courses and residential short courses which the new institution of the Open University might make in this regard. The Royal Charter of the university specifies among the objects of the institution 'to provide education of *university* and *professional* standards and to promote the educational *wellbeing of the community generally.*'

In the joint UGC/NAB statement of advice to the Secretary of State for Education in *A Strategy for Higher Education in the Late 1980s and Beyond* (NAB 1984) a new fifth objective was added to the four Robbins purposes for higher education. Robbins, as will be recalled, had spoken of instruction in skills, promotion of general powers of the mind, the advancement of learning and the transmission of a common culture and common standards of citizenship. This new fifth objective was 'the provision of continuing education in order to facilitate technological, economic and social change and to meet individual needs for personal development.'[4]

As we have seen, neither the Robbins Report nor the report of the Planning Committee for the Open University used the words continuing education as a technical descriptor in a higher education context. Nor indeed did the 1944 Education Act in the context of adult education. We might therefore be helped towards a working definition by the DES discussion paper on continuing education: *Post Experience Vocational Provision for those in Employment.*[5] This suggests that 'Initial education can be defined as the continuous preparatory period of a formal study to whatever level completed before entering main employment. Continuing education covers anything which follows.'

Another, broadly consistent line is taken in the report of the Open University's Venables Committee on Continuing Education which states, 'We have chosen to focus attention on education for adults which is normally resumed after a break or interruption – often involving a period of employment.'[6] The final report of the Advisory Council for Adult and Continuing Education *Continuing Education: from policies to practice* further stresses the potential breadth of the concept: 'Continuing education should be construed as comprising the wide range of education *and training* (my emphasis) provided for adults through the public education sector, through the vast number of statutory, voluntary and independent bodies and within industry and commerce.'[7]

However, the problem of definition clearly persists, particularly with regard to the framing of policy in higher education – as the DES working party report *The Legal Basis of Further Education* makes clear. It concluded that there should be no specific mention of *continuing* and *adult* education in any legislation. It took this view because 'both terms are imprecise and we do not believe that widely acceptable definitions can be found.' The report also contended that continuing education 'is a concept which in its broadest interpretation embraces virtually the whole of further education as it is now understood. To adopt these terms in legislation would therefore amount to tautology.'[8]

Even the UNESCO definition, comprehensive though it is, describes a process and does not easily translate into an institutional basis for policy:

> ... the entire body of educational processes whatever the content level and method, whether formal or otherwise, whether they prolong or replace initial education in schools, colleges and universities as well as in apprenticeship, whereby persons regarded as adult by the society to which they belong develop their abilities, enrich their knowledge, improve their technical or professional qualifications or turn them in a new direction and bring about changes in their attitudes or behaviour in the twofold perspective of full personal development and participation in balanced and independent social economic and cultural development.[9]

# An Alternative Basis for Policy and Principles

Faced with such an apparent absence of any current tight single definition from which one might argue for a policy or adduce a set of principles, there is a temptation to take another approach. This involves posing two basic pragmatic questions and seeing if the answers offer a means of sharpening the focus sufficiently to have a value in contributing to discussions of policy and principle. First, who is involved in the range of activities to which the classification continuing education in a higher education context currently attaches in practice? Secondly, what are the underlying reasons for the present relatively fashionable high profile concern with activities so classified as continuing education?

In adopting this approach I am indebted to the stimulus of an open lecture given by Peter Scott, editor of *The Times Higher Educational Supplement*, on the occasion of the annual residential meeting of the Open University's Council in September 1984. Having also tussled with the definition issue, he concluded that continuing education represents 'a volatile diversity determined by the accumulation of effective practice.' This diversity acknowledges that continuing education has become a part of the main stream of higher education: 'it has ceased to be extra-mural' and that liberal adult education has been eclipsed by instrumental continuing education.

Who then is involved in this activity? Scott suggests four main groups:

- mature students on undergraduate and postgraduate courses
- students on post-experience courses – either as a matter of formal professional requirement or motivated by close occupational or career development relevance
- students attending short courses – again largely with a vocational bias
- students attending 'conventional' extra-mural and adult education courses for broader purposes of self improvement or recreation.

One may wish to refine or challenge these definitions but the categories are visible and quantifiable whether from the USR, NAB planning figures or DES projections and each has a particular impact on the planning, funding and staffing of individual higher education institutions.

# Why Continuing Education?

Why then the current preoccupation with continuing education issues – in policy discussion and on paper – if not in resource allocation and practical development? Scott again suggested four triggers. First, the 'education thrives on education' effect. Are we witnessing in the current concern for continuing education the effect of Robbins on the output end of higher education in the same way as Robbins itself was a response to the output effects of the 1944 Education Act in the secondary sector? Second, the pressure for greater equality of educational opportunity. Third, the requirement for continuous re-skilling and updating of, especially but not exclusively, technological manpower. Fourth, some perceived rigidities in the existing higher education system – with regard for example to response times in introducing new degree patterns, the arts to science 'switch', some aspects of access, and an alleged resistance to change in teaching technologies.

## Educational Needs and Consequences for Policy

Does this type of analysis help us to address policy options or clarify issues of principle? I believe it may, in that the more closely we look at the educational and employment context of the four groups identified, the more clearly we perceive policy requirements which overlap departmental boundaries. For example, the evidence which ACACE (Fig.7.1) brought forward in *From Policies to Practice* on the destination of school-leavers in 1977 suggests that, given the relative lack of end-on higher and further educational opportunity, there is a current set of continuing education needs, personal, job related and technological, which affect all four groups.[10] However, in any given instance these needs may impinge on DES, DOE, DTI and in some cases DHSS interests simultaneously. Maurice Peston, in confronting this issue in the first volume of the SRHE Leverhulme Programme of Study into the Future of Higher Education, *Higher Education and the Labour Market*, added two further important interrelationships – that between central and local government and that between government, educational institutions as such and major quangos such as MSC and the University Grants Committee itself.[11] In what ways, for example, will the MSC's adult training strategy contribute to, or make demands of developing continuing educational policies in the higher education sector, and in what forum will such questions be asked and answered?

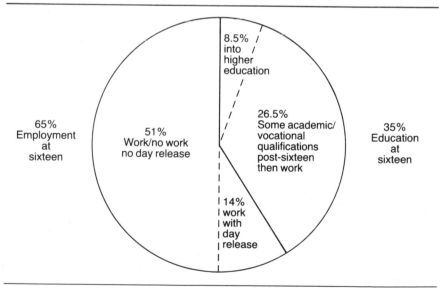

**Source**   ACACE *From Policies to Practice* p. 20.

**Figure 7.1**
Educational Destinations of School-leavers in England and Wales.

Amid this complexity what messages are there in fact for policies for continuing education in a higher education context? The earlier ACACE paper, *Adult Students and Higher Education*, suggested a number of such messages, some of which are indeed in the process of being taken up.[12] Others of them appear to languish in a kind of transbinary and inter-departmental limbo. The ACACE suggestions are essentially practical:

1 *The modification of selection procedures and criteria.* This will need to be pursued both at the point of initial entry into higher education and when continuing education opportunities are being sought after a period of employment or non-work. Such devices as profiling and tests of competences and appropriate weightings for work experience and role experience will need to be further explored and given a standing in policy terms.

2 Access mechanisms:
   a *Part-time and modular study* which can be accommodated into working and domestic life with comparatively little permanent disruption enables a broader range of participation in continuing education.
   b *Financial and social facilitation.* Mechanisms which address the issue of paid educational leave effectively, and which adequately recognize part-time study as eligible for grant, which do not discriminate against job sharing and which offer support of a practical kind for women still caring for young dependents, again serve to enhance access.

3 *Credit transfer.* The ability to acquire, stockpile and trade an educational credit currency with a wide acceptability on both sides of the binary line and to employers recognizes the often non-linear development of continuing education pathways. It allows credit to be transferred from institution to institution and sector to sector, and if fully explored offers a chance for a true currency for 'experiential' as well as educational credit.

4 *Comprehensive educational guidance services for continuing education.* Arguably one of the most economical and effective ways of maximizing continuing education opportunity – even within present policies – is the full development of an effective and comprehensive educational guidance service for adults. The models do exist, the ACACE paper *Links to Learning* identified them eloquently.[13] Yet, even since that date, far from there being a rise in this type of educational brokerage paralleling developments in the United States, a number of these inter-agency low budget endeavours have had to close for lack of resource. Furthermore, it's probably true to say that precisely because of their slim resource base, these local services have faced their strongest challenges when concerned with mature higher education entry or specialized 'in service' industrial and professional development.

# Redistribution of Resource

A case for a policy of redistribution of resources may seem to emerge from the foregoing. The ACACE paper *Adult Students and Higher Education*, on which we have just drawn, concludes with a very brief opening of the door to discussion on the economics of continuing education. It seeks to challenge the classic 'human capital theory' which has for so long ensured the loading of resource into the early phases of education – basic 'front-end' education. It suggests that there are significant risks for stagnation in professional and industrial life for those who have apparently achieved a terminal qualification at the age of 21-23. More evidence is needed to confirm or question that contention. However, the case is taken further in one of the last ACACE occasional papers to be published *Continuing Education within Universities and Polytechnics* – also published by SRHE in 1982 in Volume 6 of the Leverhulme Programme of Study into the Future of Higher Education.[14] The paper draws our attention to the other classic argument for 'front end loading' of educational resource. This is of course that *society as a whole* benefits from initial education, more than does the individual, by way of having, via initial education, citizens who are literate and numerate so as to be effective workers and to share certain patterns of thought and codes of conduct. We may question from an observation of the society about us whether this happens. If it does not happen, perhaps we should also ask whether this is because the initial education system is inefficient or because it is being asked to do the wrong things. Simply starving the initial sector of resource – whether to achieve exchequer spending cuts overall or to redistribute such resource in other sectors of education – without redefining objectives is likely to be extremely damaging. In pursuit of such a risky redefinition we may be struck by an analogy used by the Danish adult educator Werner Rasmussen:

> With more intensive adult education it may be possible to reduce the pressure on the supplies of education to adolescents and young adults. At the present time, there is everywhere a tendency to overload these supplies, because they are considered the baggage for a lifetime. We can compare it with an expedition to a big desert – tropical or arctic – where no supply stations of any kind are established. By the time it sets off on its lengthy journey to the desert the expedition must have large supplies of food and other necessities. The situation would be entirely different if there were stations or depots along the route. The lifelong journey should in the future be supported by supply stations. It will thereby be possible to travel more lightly, which means it will not be necessary to load the memories of young people so much. This will at the same time be of great value to the educational processes during these earlier years. It will be an easier task for the teachers to ensure the motivation and attention of their young students.[15]

We may find the analogy helpful or not. Herbert Strines made very precise references to the Danish, French and West German legislative moves of the late 60s and early 70s to alter the balance of educational resource distribution – and pointed out to the disadvantage of the United States of America 'an unfortunate link between our failure as an industrialized nation to compete with the rest of the world – and our failure to invest in our human resources and upgrade individuals continuously throughout their adult lives so that they can possess the skills necessary to produce and service ever more complicated products.'[16]

## Leisure Needs

However, we would be unwise to concentrate exclusively on the updating of skills within continuing education policy objectives, although this dimension has by far the greatest political impact and capacity to attract resource – witness the establishment in the UK of the Manpower Services Commission. The ACACE paper *Continuing Education within Universities and Polytechnics* reminds us in Proposition 1.5 that 'Rapid technological development both demands regular updating *and* creates more leisure. These are the two main grounds for transferring resource to continuing or post initial education.'[17] With regard to this second objective the authors go on to argue that increased leisure time will be a fact of life whether through planned reduction of the working week or involuntarily (through unemployment). They question the dismissive attitude of critics who regard continuing education in these circumstances as a mere agent of social control – a continuing education variant of 'custodial' secondary education. Their claim is that 'the imaginative use of the time freed by the advance of technology to allow students to explore knowledge in all its forms, to use information, to formulate, plan and execute community initiatives freely and openly – in short to learn to live and act within a democracy – must be viewed as an enormous potential enrichment of the individual and of society.'

## Is there a Policy Package?

Perhaps it is possible to discern from the foregoing the developing outlines of a policy package for continuing education within higher education. First, it may be characterized by the redistribution of resource between initial education and the education of adults. By 'initial' here we define both secondary education in a conventional sense but also initial higher education, and by implication will be seeking to scrutinize the kinds of transferable skills which are available to individuals at the end of either of those two phases. Second, any policy likely to be capable of delivering is almost bound to be transbinary in its nature. Recent joint UGC/NAB moves are a welcome sign of the acknowledgement of this, but there remains perhaps, particularly to do with continuing education, considerable debate as to the healthiest balance between the two transbinary partners. Third, as we have noted that the interests of several departments of government are frequently concerned in continuing education development either directly or by implication, realistic developing policies are likely to be inter-departmental. Fourth, consortial arrangements of a variety of kinds, bringing together the resources of institutions across the binary line and linking the interests of local and central government, are likely to be the vehicles for implementing and developing continuing education policy. Fifth, the relationship between current major providers of continuing education in a conventional sense and the work of major quangos such as the

MSC needs rapid further rationalization. To be effective, the Adult Training Strategy will need to involve tertiary institutions on both sides of the binary line on a basis of understanding and consent.

These broad features of policy are required to be underpinned by adequate educational guidance services. Realistic staff development policies and practices are needed within 'organizations of consent' in order to assist staff to meet the needs of new client groups. Furthermore, there will be a need to network existing resource between institutions, using the opportunities afforded by information technology in order to avoid what has been called a characteristic of the history of English higher education, namely that innovations tend to be introduced by the creation of new institutions rather than by the acceptance of innovation by existing institutions.

Finally we need to address concepts of obligation and right as they apply to these issues.

## Conceptions of Obligation and Right

Conceptions of obligation and right are not given but are sensitive to context and climate. The TUC statement *Priorities in Continuing Education* saw discussion of a comprehensive policy for continuing education as necessarily including policies designed to widen the opportunity for working people to enter higher education.[18] In concentrating on this aspect, the statement clearly acknowledged the need for new resources to be committed and advocated the right to paid educational leave as an access mechanism. Although, undoubtedly, paid educational leave is a potentially potent means of extending access, and although the Government of the day ratified International Labour Organisation Convention No.140 with regard to Paid Educational Leave, no significant advances in paid educational leave have been achieved within the UK.[19]

Maybe this is because we have in general failed to be significantly rigorous in considering issues of obligation and right. For example, is all the obligation properly to rest on the providers of continuing education. Is it sufficient to implement in full Section 41 of the 1944 Education Act and make a reality of 'the duty of every local education authority to secure the provision for their area of adequate facilities for education ...'? Or are there consequent obligations which lie with the consumer – obligations for example to contribute to current 'skills shortage' areas, to undertake to move to where jobs appropriate to their continuing education benefit are located. And what of rights? Does a right to continuing education not carry with it a right to have a voice in what is taught, how it is assessed, and where and when it is available. Furthermore, does the right itself imply for the consumer some or any of the obligations described above?

Answers to these questions are more frequently oblique and pragmatic than rooted in clear analysis. This may not be surprising, for the questions are complex and many possible answers are expensive and or unacceptable. 'Can Britain afford to create a comprehensive system of continuing education?' – asked the ACACE final report.[20] And went on to suggest that the question was more pertinent in reverse – can the country afford not to? 'The consequences of not providing a much wider and more diverse range of educational opportunities for *adults* could be serious; with a population insufficiently skilled to develop and exploit new technologies and unable to adapt to the economic and social changes produced by those technologies, with a deepening economic decline from failure to compete in world markets and with social conflict sharpening as the economy deteriorates.'

Although somewhat foreboding in tone this does not seem far away in sentiment from the 'necessary conclusion' of the final report of the Adult Education Sub-Committee of the Ministry of Reconstruction in 1919 'that adult education must not be regarded as a luxury for a few exceptional persons here and there, nor as a thing which concerns only a short span of early manhood, but that it is a permanent national necessity, an inseparable aspect of citizenship and therefore should be both universal and lifelong.'[21]

Both statements seem to share common elements of a recurring theme to which we seem nationally resistant.

Back in 1976, in their campaigning tract *Right to Learn – the case for adult equality*, Rogers and Groombridge argued to good effect that the hardly tapped capacity of adults to learn is 'our most neglected political, social and economic resource.'[22] Almost a decade later there is still much to be done to remedy this neglect – perhaps particularly in the context of formal higher education. The facilities it requires are not yet in place. But the price for any remedy may be high, the more so as the total size of the educational cake remains limited. Perhaps the hard question is best and most sharply put by the authors of the ACACE paper *Continuing Education within Universities and Polytechnics* who suggest that the strongest test of one's commitment to the idea of a right to more continuing education lies in whether one can answer yes to the following question – 'If no more money in total were available for education as a whole, would you be willing to accept a redistribution of resources; one which, say, gave relatively less to 18-21 year-olds so that older and part-time students could have better access and provision?'[23]

# References

1  Robbins, Lord (1963) *Report of the Committee on Higher Education under the Chairmanship of Lord Robbins* Cmnd 2154
2  Open University (1969) *Report of the Planning Committee for the Open University to the Secretary of State for Education and Science* HMSO
3  Swann, M. (1968) *The Flow into Employment of Scientists, Engineers and Technologists* Report of the Committee on Manpower Resources in Science and Technology. Cmnd 3760
4  National Advisory Body (1984) *A Strategy for Higher Education in the late 1980s and Beyond*
5  DES (1980) *Continuing Education: Post-experience Vocational Provision for those in Employment*
6  Venables, P.(1976) *Report of the Committee on Continuing Education in the Open University* Milton Keynes: Open University
7  ACACE (1982) *Continuing Education: from policies to practice*
8  DES (1981) *The Legal Basis of Further Education*
9  Titmus, C. et al. (1979) *Terminology of Adult Education* UNESCO
10  ACACE *op. cit.*

11  Lindley, R. (Ed.) (1981) *Higher Education and the Labour Market* Guild-ford: SRHE

12  ACACE (1979) *Adult Students and Higher Education*

13  ACACE (1979) *Links to Learning* Report on educational information, advisory and counselling services for adults

14  ACACE (1983) *Continuing Education within Universities and Polytechnics*

15  Rasmussen, W. (1970) *Permanent Education* Council of Europe

16  Strines, Herbert E. (1972) *Continuing Education as a National Capital Investment* Upjohn Institute

17  ACACE (1983) *op. cit.*

18  TUC (1978) *Priorities in Continuing Education*

19  Charnley, A. (1975) *Paid Educational Leave* Hart-Davis Educational

20  ACACE (1982) *op. cit.*

21  Ministry of Reconstruction (1919) *Report of the Adult Education sub-committee of the Ministry of Reconstruction* Nottingham University Press (1980)

22  Rogers, J. and Groombridge, B. (1976) *Right to Learn* Arrow

23  ACACE (1983) *op. cit.*

# 8

# A Case in the Motor Industry

## R.A. Shepherd

If this were to be a sermon, I would want to take as my text 'If you think training is expensive, try ignorance.' This text is one which the training fraternity in Ford quote whenever we are asked to justify to outsiders the extent and the cost of the training we do. I say 'to outsiders', because within the Company the question does not really need to be asked. To those who are footing the bill, the need for training is self-evident, and we find it difficult, as a company, to understand why any other organization which is operating in a highly competitive market would take a contrary view.

However, it appears that in this respect what is good for Ford does not appear to be good for the nation! The Government and the Manpower Services Commission have certainly believed for a long time that the amount of vocational education and training undertaken in Britain lags far behind all our major competitors. Indeed, Geoffrey Holland, the director of the MSC, has gone as far as to say that not only are we not in the same league as our competitors, we are not even in the same game. This may be somewhat 'over the top', but the message is quite clear – that unless we can somehow match the performance of West Germany, Japan and the United States in vocational education and training, we shall continue to fail to match them in overall economic performance. Nevertheless, I believe that British industry may be guilty of underselling itself. For example, we have recently undertaken a broad review of our own expenditure on education and training and it matches the West German rate that was quoted in the National Economic Development Organisation/Manpower Services Commission report *Competence and Competition*. Although I am prepared to accept that large company experience such as ours may not be typical of the economy as a whole, I believe that more training – and certainly more *learning* – is going on than employers are given credit for.

Having said that, and recognizing that what we do in Ford may *not* be typical of British industry, I believe it may still be helpful to describe, in broad terms, what we are doing. Before that, however, I want to spend a few moments painting in the backcloth. A Financial Times survey of the motor industry showed that it is a fiercely competitive industry and that those of us competing in it are feeling a good deal of strain, not to say pain. Ford is quoted as calculating that the European industry made a combined loss of $2.1 billion between 1978 and 1981 and another $1.2 billion in 1982 and 1983.

There is close to a 20% over-capacity in vehicle manufacturing, which is not helped by the policy of a number of states supporting and even financially underpinning home-based manufacturers. Japanese makers have taken about one million car sales in Europe from the domestic producers and have also eliminated about 1.6 million vehicles which European manufacturers previously exported. Not only is this creating a problem here and now, it means that the future is also looking bleak because not only will the Japanese continue to be a major threat, but it is most unlikely that governments will allow home-based manufacturers to fail, which means that the rest of us will have to fight even harder to retain our place in the market.

All this means a tremendous pressure to improve manufacturing productivity, to reduce fixed costs and to re-examine the way in which the industry is currently organized and administered. In these circumstances it would not be surprising if one of our responses to cutting fixed costs were to cut back on training. 'Not surprising', because if one believes the evidence of the MSC and others, cutting back on training is the typical 'kneejerk' response of employers in times of crisis.

But, as I have indicated already, this has *not* been the response within my own Company. There has never been a time in my thirty-five years' experience when we have been so heavily engaged in training and retraining. Let me deal first with what I call the comparatively straightforward aspects of this training effort – that which has been made in response to the demands of advanced technology.

No one is going to gasp with amazement when I say that the micro-chip is well on the way to revolutionizing how we design and make and sell vehicles and how we administer a complex commercial organization. What may be surprising, however, is that, with the exception of its impact on office administration, the introduction of the micro-chip is only the latest in a long line of technological advances with which employees have had to become familiar. When I joined the Company in 1950, Ford was just installing its first automatic cylinder block transfer line, in which cylinder blocks were moved from station to station and a variety of machining operations undertaken automatically. If you had walked into our body plants in recent years you would have seen – and can still see – complex multi-welders which instantaneously spot weld with accuracy and high quality a complete body shell.

The list is almost endless of the ways in which increasingly complex technology has gradually transformed our business, and at all times these advances have meant that employees have needed to be trained in the use of the new equipment, whether as operators or as maintenance employees. Here a key point to make is that no changes to product or manufacturing processes are made without a clear analysis of what is proposed. This invariably involves a formal procedure such as a Project Request, leading to funding approval. Those responsible for implementing the change and its outcome are also involved in the project planning and are required to sign off and indicate approval. This would, of course, include any inherent training requirements that such a project might create.

Line management, amongst its other roles, has to meet the learning needs of the people for whom it has responsibility. This role is often invisible to others, because much of it is excercised through telling, selling, instruction, demonstration, coaching and counselling. When the changes involve radical new methods, procedures, knowledge and skills, it becomes necessary formally to invoke specialist training. Such needs are normally perceivable at the time of planning, with formal provision made for them, including finance, lead time and the identification of potential training resources. It is the function of personnel and training staff to advise line management about such provision.

Now, of course, the robot, whether for spot welding or paint spraying, or for positioning components in machines is commonplace. And its widescale introduction has created an enormous training need among our maintenance employees in particular. Although the robot is essentially a mechanical piece of equipment it is controlled electronically as are so many pieces of equipment these days. The need for training in electronics and fluid logic (even hydraulic control equipment is now based on computer logic) has been growing for a number of years and the introduction of robots with their programmable controllers, has accelerated this demand to the point where even our expanded internal resources are no longer able to cope with the pressure of work. We have, therefore, had to rely on external agencies.

The changes have affected, too, our training of apprentices and this is where the three- to four-year lead time required to train an apprentice has proved to be a problem. One of my Centres had recently to take back for retraining some recently completed toolmaker apprentices in order to convert them into machine maintenance fitters, because demand for toolmakers had declined in the interim. Another sign of the times has been an almost total reversal of the traditional need for mechanically trained, as opposed to electrically trained apprentices. At our Halewood Centre, for example, of 1984's intake of thirty apprentices, twenty-two were electricians. Not only does this call for a fundamental change in the training programme, but it means we also have to retrain some of our instructors, whose existing skills naturally reflect the previous mechanical dominance.

Computer aided design is also creating an enormous new training workload and brings into question the way in which we educate and train engineers at all levels. It is doubtful if we shall ever again require draughtsmen of the traditional kind and certainly not in the numbers we have hitherto trained. The technicians we recruit now need to be capable of absorbing the higher academic content which high technology demands; it is the same with our professional engineers and technicians in manufacturing. The totally new processes by which vehicles are now manufactured are placing heavy demands on the skills and knowledge of our traditionally educated and trained manufacturing and plant engineers, and massive retraining is essential if they are to continue to make an effective contribution to our production capability.

Finally, in this catalogue of change, are the office areas, and it is possible to argue that the impact of advanced technology has been more sudden and dramatic in the offices than it has been in the factories. Within the space of only two or three years, almost every desk in every office has acquired its own micro-computer and, as is the way with such things, there has not been a common hardware adopted for all systems. There has, therefore, been the problem, not only of introducing office workers to the computers, but also of ensuring that we can train them in a variety of hardware and software systems. Again, to meet this comparatively sudden and massive demand, we have augmented internal facilities by bringing in a variety of external trainers.

We have extensive reference files on such agencies, but more than that, we have discussions with many of them if we believe they might be helpful as an alternative or an addition to existing resources. We favour courses tailor-made to our needs, but there are occasions on which we might compromise our ideal solution with what is available 'off the shelf'. However, we do this as infrequently as possible. The agencies we use vary widely, and they include colleges of further education, polytechnics, skill centres, private training services, etc. In some circumstances, when requiring medium-term updating in special techniques, say finite element analysis or other complex and mathematical procedures, we have bought in tailor-made courses from universities.

Currently, for example, we have contracted with a number of academic establishments to help us run Statistical Process Control training for our suppliers. This has involved us in training in our own Centre the academic staff concerned, in order that they may become familiar with the objectives and methodology. Otherwise, the proportion of bought-in training from universities and polytechnics is limited. It tends to be for specific update requirement for existing qualified engineers. For the lower level needs of technicians and craftsmen, we find that local colleges collaborate with us very satisfactorily.

As I hinted earlier, I am sure that none of this is strange to anyone and I take no particular pride in outlining what we are doing. What it does say, however, loudly and clearly, is that without an enormous training effort over the past few years, we could not have responded effectively to the opportunities provided by the introduction of new technology. At a rough estimate, the short training courses which employees have attended have involved about one in five of them for an average time of about four days. No one doubts, though, that the high cost of providing this training is vastly outweighed by the benefits it has brought in enabling the Company to improve individual productivity.

Incidentally, because training has been an integral element in keeping pace with technological change over many years, employees have never resisted it or used it as a bargaining ploy, as has happened with some 'new technology' agreements.

Turning now to a different pressure on our human resource, let me say a few words about the constant need, in the face of the competition I have talked about, to become a more efficient organization in *every* way. It is well known that one of the factors which has made British industry uncompetitive has been its over-manning and its top-heavy management structures, and one of the significant aspects of recent years has been the way in which British industry has become leaner.

In our own Company we have shed over 20% of our employees since 1979, a pattern that has been repeated across industry. In becoming leaner, it is necessary to look at the way the Company is organized. Is the organizational structure cost-effective? Are there too many layers of management? Are we, paradoxically, over-controlled, in that line managers are not given enough authority and staff activities are thus inflated? All these are questions which have to be addressed, particularly knowing how much lower the manning levels are in all functions in Japanese industry. Our response has been to cut out layers of management and to combine activities to reduce the superstructure. Earlier on I mentioned, for example, the Japanese impact on our export markets. It is not surprising, therefore, to learn that we have had to reshape our export organization to reflect this and to redeploy many of those previously engaged in export work.

The training implications of all this are fairly clear. Any major reshuffle of activities or responsibilities creates a learning need. I can speak with personal knowledge. For example, a manager from one of our export sales activities is now running our Mode A Youth Training Scheme. Another took over in late 1984 from the retiring manager of my technical education and training activity. Some years ago, a surplus production superintendent took over the Halewood Technical Training Centre when its supervisor retired. We retrained and redeployed those of our foundry employees, including management, who did not either retire or take voluntary redundancy. Again, the catalogue of learning needs is almost endless.

What all this has done is to change the whole basis upon which we used to develop our employees, particularly in management. When we were an expanding organization – throughout the 1950s and 60s and early in the 1970s – managers were developed by what we would call experiential learning. Formal training was minimal and we were the bane of all external training consultants! Job movement, sideways and upwards, under close supervision, guaranteed that young people acquired knowledge, skills and experience to prepare them for higher level jobs within their particular functions. Cross-functional movement was the exception rather than the rule and so there was no requirement to learn totally new disciplines.

This has now all changed. We are a contracting organization under severe pressure and the need to make the best use of our human resources is greater than ever. This need was finally recognized in 1980 when we opened our first Management and Staff Training Centre, a modest, non-residential facility which very quickly proved to be totally inadequate in terms of its size and staffing to meet the demand, which has since grown almost exponentially. Some years ago we revolutionized the training of our first line shop floor supervision, which was the target population we first identified as being in need of new skills to manage the new circumstances; and the story since then has been that more and more line managers in other functions have recognized the need for these skills in themselves and their subordinates if they are to come to grips with the problems of managing in an environment of rapid change.

This brings me to the last, and, to me, possibly the most exciting development which is occurring in my Company and one which presents totally new demands on our training resources. There has been a gradual realization in the past few years that to match the Japanese in technology is not enough. Part of the success of the Japanese industry lies in cultural differences and in the management processes which stem from those cultural differences. Ironically, it was the United States car industry which was probably among the first to recognize and respond to this, importing what the US had originally exported to postwar Japan! From 1979 to 1982, the US car industry went through the worst recession it had experienced since the 1930s and, in the view of many, this was not simply a more dramatic example of the normal cyclical experience of the industry which would revert to normal in due course. It was recognized that in order to match the challenge of the Japanese in terms of productivity, quality and cost, simply waiting for the good times to return was not going to save them. A much more radical change was needed in the way business was done.

In Ford US this took the form of an historic agreement with the Union of Automobile Workers in 1979, in which the Union and the Company agreed jointly to set-up and administer an employee involvement programme. Without going into too much detail, it involved the creation of joint Company/Union steering committees at national and plant level and problem-solving work groups run by the employees themselves, in which they, for the first time, other than through the bargaining process, were able to make an impact on decisions affecting their jobs. The evidence so far suggests that – with a few hiccups – improvement in quality, working practices and day-to-day employee relations has been marked.

In training terms what did this mean? Well, for the first time, the need was identified to help employees at all levels operate a group approach to problems in which consensus was the only way forward. The impact of this on a management and workforce used to a confrontational environment was clearly enormous. The Company had very quickly to mount and sustain training programmes in the whole range of skills required to ensure that their Employee Involvement (EI) programme could operate effectively.

Since this was a Company/Union agreement, covering only manual workers, salaried employees and management generally were not covered by it. New means had to be found to respond to the interest shown by non-Union and management employees. This was launched in one of the Company's major divisions, as the Participative Management (PM) programme. In the jargon, EI and PM are seen to be two sides of the same coin. In both of them, similar kinds of skills are required by those participating. But more than this was needed, because the Participative Management programme is essentially an organizational development programme in which the management teams concerned are aiming to change the culture of their organization and to manage it in a different way.

As is often the way with such things, we in the United Kingdom have been looking at the United States experience and seeing whether we can emulate it. Unfortunately, the manual unions in the United Kingdom have not yet felt able to follow the example of their American colleagues, for reasons which are understandable, even if, in my view, misguided. The staff unions, on the other hand, have taken a slightly more positive view and, following a visit of a number of staff representatives to the United States in August, signed an agreement with the Company in February 1985, so that an Employee Involvement programme might be launched. At senior management level we have run two Participative Management seminars, and I have been fortunate enough to have been personally involved in helping to run several recently for our truck organization. What is significant about all these efforts is that we are looking at *groups* of employees, whether at shop floor level or within the management structure, not simply at employees as individuals. This alone is having, and will continue to have, a major impact on our training activity. Our Management Staff Training Centre, for example, runs programmes which are essentially for 'stranger' groups, not for 'family' groups. We have recognized that we may need to rethink what we are offering because 'stranger' group training, however effective at the individual level, cannot address the problems of making work groups more effective.

As I have said, this most recent development is, for me, probably the most exciting development I have seen in my career with the Company. This is not to down-grade in any way the need for, or the competence with which we have undertaken technical training or the enormous strides forward we have made in formal management training. But technical competence alone is not likely to save us. We must move into an era where the organization as a whole, and major components within it, are operating more effectively as a team. This obviously applies to the shop floor employees and their supervision, but is also very important in all other activities within a complex organization such as ours.

Summarizing then, Ford has, apparently contrary to national experience, been increasing its training effort enormously over the past five years, not only in response to the imperatives of advanced technology; not only to meet the needs for organizational effectiveness brought about by structural changes within the organization; but also by recognizing the need for new ways of achieving organizational goals by developing the effectiveness of work teams at all levels. Unless those responsible recognize the need to develop to the full their human resources, they will all too quickly learn the truth of the text with which I began. 'If you think training (or perhaps I should substitute 'learning') is expensive, try ignorance.'

# Note

This article was based on a paper presented at the National Conference of the Institute of Personnel Management held at Harrogate in October 1984.

# 9

# The Case in
# Three European Countries

*Colin Titmus*

Anyone who has taken the trouble to get to know continuing education in advanced countries outside the United Kingdom will find there familiar phenomena, as well as strange ways of doing things. They may also find that a study of foreign practice, what is done, how, who pays for it, what is the thinking behind it, may offer a wider perspective upon British practice. It may help determine how peculiar is the United Kingdom situation and thus how valid it is to seek solutions only within British experience, what elements, if any, the British experience shares with other countries and how relevant what they do is to us.

This chapter tries to provide some information which may help to answer such questions in relation to the continuing education activities of higher education in three European countries. A broad general survey of advanced countries was rejected because it would inevitably have been superficial in this space. Certain aspects of provision in France, West Germany and Sweden have been chosen because of the interest of the aspects themselves and because the societies in which they occur are, like the United Kingdom, advanced European industrial nations, with marked individual national characteristics, but sharing a number of basic traditions of thought and behaviour and subject to many similar social, cultural, economic and political influences.

## Tradition and change in university adult education in Western Europe

Thirty years ago representatives of universities on the mainland of Europe could deny that their institutions had any duties to the communities in which they existed.[1] In the years since then their tradition of detachment from the world around them, of concern to teach only knowledge they generated themselves to a small social and intellectual élite, on terms dictated by the academics, has been seriously undermined. In the name of social justice Western European universities have had to accept that they were required to teach a mass student body on terms in the fixing of which society, or the state as its voice, would have a major say. On the one hand social insistence that any individual had the right to reach his or her full educational potential, on the other hand society's need for specific knowledge and skills and for their continual updating have exerted a significant influence on what higher education should teach and for what purpose. A state requires that its citizens have continuing access to the means of renovating and extending what they know and can do. Institutions of higher education are the places where the newest and most complex knowledge can most easily be made available. They must therefore be opened to all those people whom society requires to have this knowledge. Western European institutions of higher education have been under pressure to change quite radically and, among other new responsibilities, to undertake a commitment to continuing education.

## University Continuing Education in France

Student discontents, pent up over years, lay behind the riots of 1968, which almost brought down the French government. Without that shock to the State and the higher education system it is doubtful whether the major reforms embodied in the Law of 12 November 1968 on the Direction of Higher Education would have reached the statute book. Among its other innovations it provided the legal basis for continuing education in French higher education.

Before it there had been, it is true, some initiatives by a few individuals. For example, several universities had Institutes of Labour, which offered courses to trade unionists, and at Nancy the Advanced School of Mines had a prestigious National Institute of Adult Education (INFA). The 1968 Law set out to impose a general obligation. Article 1 stated:

> Higher education must be open to former students as well as people who have not had the opportunity to pursue studies in order to allow them, according to their ability, to improve their chances of promotion or to change their occupational activity.
> Universities must co-operate, particularly by making use of the new means of diffusing knowledge, in lifelong education for the use of all categories of the population and for all the purposes it may include.

Universities were to be opened to adults without formal qualifications so that they could follow award-bearing courses. Appropriate teaching methods were to be devised and the university was to liaise with outside organizations in the development of continuing education.[2]

At first nothing happened. In France, legislation such as the 1968 Law is largely a statement of intent, it requires ministerial orders and decrees to spell out in detail what shall be done, and how, before it can be implemented. Other reforms in the government and organization of higher education went ahead, but in itself the 1968 Law only changed the climate of continuing education. Not until the much wider Law of 1971 Relating to the Organization of Continuing Vocational Education within the Framework of Lifelong Education was anything practical done.[3]

The 1971 Law, also largely a product of the events of 1968, provided the framework within which continuing education, whether vocational or non-vocational, has operated in France ever since. It began:

> Permanent vocational education constitutes a national obligation. The object is to permit the adaptation of workers to change in techniques and conditions of work to encourage their social advancement by access to different levels of culture and professional qualification and their contribution to cultural, economic and social development.

It created a free market to meet this obligation, in accordance with the economic principles of the government of the time. Those requiring training schemes were at liberty to commission any person or organization offering to provide training and to pay them from continuing education funds under fixed contract. In addition to public educational establishments, specifically listed as having a role in this process, either as clients or *providers*, were 'Firms, groups of firms, private establishments and bodies, professional, trade union and family organizations, local authorities, public establishments, particularly chambers of commerce and industry, chambers of trade and chambers of agriculture.' There would be some contribution from the State, but continuing education would be principally financed by a tax on all private employers having at least ten employees, calculated as a percentage of their annual wage bill. (It stands currently at 1.2%.) Any expenditure incurred by an employer in providing continuing education would be deducted from the tax to be paid, a measure which encouraged employers to sponsor or provide education for their own workforce and gave them a large degree of control over the market.

In order to encourage universities to enter into this market and to fulfil their obligations under the 1968 Law a circular was issued by the Ministry of Education in 1972.[4] It offered to any university which wished to apply for it a contract of initial assistance for one year to finance the creation of a Mission of Continuing Education, headed by a delegate or director. Its function would be to: '... analyse the needs of its surrounding area, to plan the resources of the university, to negotiate contracts with its external partners and to establish a coherent programme of activities.'

Specified as non-renewable, the Ministry aid was intended as a pump-priming operation, after which missions were presumably to subsist on what could be made out of training contracts – an uncertain prospect. Nevertheless, universities took up the offer in large numbers. As the contract of initial assistance did prove insufficient to establish a permanent base, it *was* renewed. By a process of transformation it has become a contract of continuing assistance, to provide a guaranteed financial foundation for the missions, which now have the generic title of the University Continuing Education Service (SUFCO). By 1980 an official guide could list seventy-two university institutions which had established formal structures to promote continuing education.[5]

That there were so many was partly due to new creations and partly to the division of large institutions into establishments of more manageable size. The University of Paris, for example, was split into thirteen. There is no binary system for France. Foundations similar in purpose to British polytechnics exist, but they are called University Institutes of Technology (IUT) and they are constituent parts of universities.

The 1968 Law both democratized and decentralized the administration of higher education, giving to individual institutions a freedom to order their own affairs which they had not previously enjoyed. This and variations in the local market account for the wide differences in the nature and extent of continuing education provision. There are, however, broad similarities in its organization. The SUFCO, under whatever name it goes, is a central service of the university, normally but not invariably under a management committee composed of representatives of academic departments and sometimes of representatives of employers and employees and other local interests. The permanent staff is small, usually fewer than half a dozen. It may do some teaching, but its principal function is organization, promotion and liaison, within and without the university. Planning and teaching of courses is the responsibility of academic departments. Most SUFCO serve a whole university, but a number of IUT and other specialized institutes run their own continuing education service, as for example at Aix-Marseille III.

Not every discipline or field of study taught within a university is available to continuing education students. Nevertheless most advertise a wide range of possibilities which can be made available if a demand exists. In France, conventional university courses lead to State recognized and regulated degrees and diplomas; these alone have legal status. A minority are advertised as open to continuing education students, and they mostly lead to occupational qualifications. A few national degree or diploma courses have been adapted to meet the needs of adults. The University of Aix-Marseille III, for example, offers first-degree and Masters courses in law. In the majority of institutions, however, only sub-degree courses (usually two years full-time) leading to the University Diploma in Technology (DUT) or the Diploma in General University Studies (DEUG) have been so adapted. On the other hand individual universities have created their own diplomas, with de facto if not de jure status, specifically for continuing education: among many others are diplomas in local administration, company management, Portuguese, human ecology, applied and theoretical photography, for animal laboratory technicians and for managers of ski schools.

Any person who has passed the Baccalaureat, the senior secondary leaving examination, has the right of entry to higher education. Without it entry has traditionally been very difficult. A few courses are now open to people with relevant work experience and many institutions offer courses leading to the Special Entry Examination to the University (ESEU), which is designed for adults.

A large number of courses leading to named awards are held in the evening or at weekends. However, the legal right of workers to long-term leave from work for study, which was enshrined in the 1971 Law and has since been modified (1978) in order to make it easier for individuals to take advantage of it, has encouraged establishments to offer full-time continuing education courses leading to degrees and diplomas.

Much of the SUFCO effort is directed to courses not leading to an award, but tailored to the social, economic and cultural requirements of the region. Courses are negotiated with individual firms or public administrations, or the SUFCO itself initiates courses designed to appeal to a number of firms or local interests. Those of the first type are for the most part specifically vocational in character, but courses in written and oral expression are not uncommon and there are others of non-vocational interest. The producers of Perrier Water negotiated with Montpellier III a course in the old regional language, Occitan. Those of the second type tend to be more general. They include courses in languages or for workers in the caring professions. Within the framework of the 1971 Law the State offers direct subsidies for courses of education aimed at specific social categories: for instance, for women wishing to return to work and for the unemployed, particularly the young. Some SUFCO organize provision for these and also work with universities of the third age.

The only limits to the level of education offered are set by each university itself and by the market. There are courses in literacy and basic education as well as in postgraduate studies, but it is probably true to say that the public served is mainly at the level of the Baccalaureat and above: executives, professionals, technicians and skilled workers. The proportion of unemployed is high, up to 50% in some cases. Although universities make available many opportunities for long-term study, short courses (under 120 hours) form the largest part of provision. The funding is varied. The operating budget derives in very large part from the provisions of the 1971 Law, either directly from the State, or from contracts signed with public or private employers, or from student fees, which may be met by the individual or by his or her employer.

The scale of continuing education activity also varies considerably. In 1978 the University of Nice had 17,000 conventional students and 1,636 in continuing education. Comparative figures for Paris VII were 35,000 and 3,700, for Grenoble II 11,000 and 4,872, for Saint Etienne 6,642 and 2,822, for Chambéry (Savoy) 2,540 and 1,225. If any generalizations can be made, they are that the smaller and newer the institution the greater proportionally is likely to be its continuing education provision and that the number of continuing education participants is usually equal to between 10% and 20% of conventional students.

# Higher Education after World War II in the Federal German Republic

After the Second World War the occupying powers in what was to become the Federal Republic of Germany took a number of steps to ensure that Nazism should never revive and that central government in West Germany should remain weak. As a result the FRG became a federal state (not, as in France, a unitary one), in which authority over education lay with the governments of the ten provinces, plus West Berlin, of which the Federation was composed. The higher education system, in spite of American efforts to democratize it, reverted at German insistence to the pre-Nazi pattern of independent institutions, ruled by a self-perpetuating oligarchy of professors and serving a small élite, in which lecturers taught what they liked and students studied what they wished.

In the 1960s and 1970s, under similar pressures to those exerted in France and other European countries, higher education in the Federal Republic was obliged to expand, to adapt what was taught more to national needs and to adopt a more democratic form of government. The necessity to take measures at national rather than provincial level in order to meet rapid economic, technological and social changes led the Federal Government to acquire more power for itself. It now has, for example, the authority to make general rules of principle regarding institutions of higher education and it may collaborate with the provisional governments in the planning and financing of existing institutions and the construction of new ones. With new foundations and with the official inclusion of advanced technical colleges, teacher training colleges and colleges of specialized professional training in the higher education sector, the membership of the West German Vice-Chancellor's Conference increased from thirty in the mid-1960s to 156 in 1983.[6]

## Legislation of Continuing Education in West German Higher Education

As part of the reforms higher education was given a legal duty to provide continuing education. The participation of universities in this was not unprecedented. There had been some examples before the First World War, and the British Occupation authorities had tried to encourage it after World War II. Although the response to the latter initiative had been small, there had been slow growth in the 1950s and 1960s, which has now been accelerated by two things. In 1973 the Joint Federal/Provincial Commission for Educational Planning produced a General Plan for Education, which laid down the following tasks for continuing education in higher education:

- collaboration with other continuing education institutions to cover the general demand for academic continuing education
- activities outside the higher education institution for higher education graduates in specialized subjects
- systematic and permanently regulated studies within the higher education institution for higher education graduates.

In 1976 the Federal Government's General Outline Law for Higher Education stated that such studies should also be open to applicants 'who have acquired the necessary aptitude for participation in their occupation or in other ways.' It required that 'experience in occupational practice be used in teaching' and that 'the needs for participation arising from occupational practice should be taken into consideration.'[7] These principles were given practical effect through subsequent provincial legislation.

The other institutions with which higher education was to collaborate were numerous and well funded, for the pre-Nazi tradition of adult education had been revived and developed from the beginnings of the Federal Republic. The main providers were and are the evening folk high schools, whose nearest British equivalent is the evening institute, but Catholic and Protestant churches, trade unions and employers' and professional organizations run their own considerable programmes.[8] Higher education was to contribute its competence in the field of course content, the adult education bodies had the expertise in programme planning, course structure and knowledge of the target public.

Higher education's own provision was clearly to be in post-experience study at graduate level, but it was intended to be open to all those who could profit from it. In that and by its vocational and practical orientation it could be an expression of higher education's sense of social responsibility.

## Provision in West German Higher Education

Only the laws of Lower Saxony and the Rhineland Palatinate specify the institutional form that continuing education shall take in higher education. Only twenty-eight, less than a fifth of the member institutions of the Vice-Chancellors' Conference, have centres specially set up to be responsible for continuing education. Most of the others engage in it, but it is a function of faculties, academic departments or committees, or is run through the central administration of the institution.[9] Where there are continuing education centres with specialist staff, they are normally responsible to the central administration. Most of them were created in new higher education foundations. Their staff rarely number more than half a dozen; they do some teaching, but are mostly concerned with promotion and administration. The greater part of the teaching is done by members of academic departments.

Data concerning the range and level of continuing education in the higher education sector is hard to come by. A report on continuing education centres showed that in 1982 they offered 1,311 short courses of up to 40 hours without formal entry conditions. Of subject-based courses (the majority), 40% were in arts subjects and 30% each in mathematics/science and social sciences. There were also a large number of cross-disciplinary and problem-oriented ones. Twenty-eight other specialized courses of varying lengths of up to 500 hours, sometimes over a period of several years, were offered. For admission to 25% of these, university entrance qualifications were required, and to 66% appropriate work experience. A few led to certificates awarded by the university responsible. A few centres operate as study centres of Federal Germany's counterpart to the Open University, the Distance University of Hagen. Others use teaching materials produced there.[10]

The great majority (around 70%) of activities in which continuing education centres were engaged originated from an initiative of the centre. Only about 30% were a response to outside demand or to findings of market research. Most activities were offered in the evenings or at weekends. There were a number of courses lasting one week of continuous attendance, in connection with which it is not without significance that several provinces have legislation conferring upon working people the right to paid educational leave of up to five or ten days every year or every other year.

For those who wish to improve their formal educational qualifications there is in Federal Germany a well-established structure of second-chance education. Adults may progress through evening academic and technical secondary schools to qualify for university entrance, and some higher education institutions provide access courses for the same purpose. There is, however, little attempt in degree or diploma teaching to meet the special needs of adults. Some continuing education centres consider it a major element of their work to study and teach adult education as a discipline, with the objective, among others, of influencing higher education practice in general, but there is little sign yet of any effect.

The responsibility for implementing the policies set out in the General Plan for Education and the General Outline Law for Higher Education lies with the provinces, but the Federal Government may sponsor experimental or pilot projects to encourage developments of the kind proposed. Many, if not most, continuing education centres in higher education institutions were originally created and financed in this way. On the expiry of the project their running costs and staff salaries have been financed out of the general budget of the institution under the various provincial laws. Activities are funded out of student fees and, to some extent, out of payments for specific provision from professional and commercial associations.

In the Federal Republic of Germany, as in France, an overall sketch of the continuing education provision made in higher education is inevitably an over-simplification. There is considerable diversity, in the extent of commitment to continuing education, in the nature of provision, its purpose and target population. Among the factors influencing this are the many different kinds of institution in the higher education sector, the age of the institution and its attachment to tradition, provincial education policy, and the still considerable freedom of each institution to do what it considers fit. In the University of Mannheim (Baden Württemberg), for example, 'study contents are marked by a high degree of abstraction', they reflect the latest state of knowledge in practice related matters and 'this claim determines the standard and hence the potential participants....' On the other hand, the objectives of the University of Oldenburg (Lower Saxony) are to make accessible to the public the knowledge pursued in the university, to make learning available to anybody interested, regardless of formal qualifications.[11] For the most part, however, continuing education is aimed at those meeting university entrance requirements or having equivalent occupational qualifications. For all its variations, continuing education in higher education in the Federal Republic has hitherto been on a small scale, but according to a recent report of the Working Groups of University Adult Education most institutions have specific plans for its expansion.[12]

# The Case of Sweden

Sweden is a different case from France, the Federal German Republic or the United Kingdom. Its area is large, but it has only 8.3 million people. It avoided the upheavals of Word War II and the social stresses that went with it. For over forty years, up to the mid-1970s, one party, the Social Democrats, remained in power. It has a homogeneous population and through a system of sustained discussion of major public decisions it has become a consensus society. After World War II it became rich, and this, together with its stability, were potent enabling factors in the most far-reaching democratization in Western Europe, carried out without the social stresses other countries had to bear.

Step by step, over a period of forty years, the Swedish education system has been fundamentally reorganized. In the 1960s the period of compulsory school attendance was raised to nine years, from the age of 7 to the age of 16, with the intention that all young people should in fact attend school until they were 19. By 1975 80% were staying on beyond the age of 16. With the care for social justice which has marked the reforms and a concern to bridge the gap between generations, free secondary education was made available to adults, over 200,000 of whom now participate in it annually.

The inevitable consequence of secondary expansion was increased pressure on places in higher education. Moreover, the logic of inter-generational equality of opportunity required that adults should have chances of higher education comparable with those which were being offered to young people. As the effects of secondary reform became apparent and the demands for a highly trained workforce grew, it became clear that the Swedish higher education system was inadequate to meet the demands made upon it. There had been some changes in the 1960s, but in 1968 the Government initiated a series of inquiries and a process of public debate, the outcome of which was the 1977 higher education law, the basis of the present reformed system.

Swedish universities had belonged firmly to the European tradition of élitist, independent institutions, detached from the society in which they existed and from the many other post-secondary institutions, which prepared people for a range of occupations. Any person who had passed the secondary leaving examination was entitled to a university place, except in vocationally oriented fields such as medicine or law, in which a numerus clausus operated. There was no time limit on study, a student presented himself for an examination when he felt ready and reached his degree by cumulation of examination credits. Since these credits were never lost, people could drop out from study and return later to take up where they had left off. Relationships between teachers and taught were usually restricted to presence at lectures.

Now the whole of higher education has been reorganized into a State sector, composed of thirty-two universities and colleges, and a municipal one, which mainly consists of healthcare institutions. For planning and allocation of funds the country comes under six regional boards, each responsible for all the higher education establishments in its area and answerable to the National Board of Universities and Colleges (UHÄ) or the National Board of Education (for municipal colleges).

The freedom to choose what to teach and what to study has been severely curtailed. Individual courses may not have clear occupational relevance, but the combination of courses in a study programme 'should constitute a good preparation for future occupational activities.'[13] Study content is divided into five lines, technology, administration, care, teaching and culture, and at institutional level Boards of Studies determine the curriculum in each one.

Entry is no longer open to all who have reached certain standards. Student numbers are limited, both overall and for each study line, and places are allocated according to a set formula. There are four quotas for places and an applicant applies under one or more of these:

1 For those who have the higher secondary leaving certificate roughly equivalent to A level.

2 For those who have a secondary leaving certificate roughly equivalent to O level.

3 For those who have completed a residential Folk High School course.

4 For those aged 25 or more, who have 4 years' work experience (including care of their family) and who take a scholastic aptitude test.

In quotas 1, 2, 3, applicants receive points according to the grades they receive and they are awarded further points for work experience. With the reservation that 30% of places are reserved for quota 1, places are allocated to quotas according to the proportion of applicants in each one.

The effect of these measures has been to open higher education widely to adults. Their take-up of the opportunities offered has been facilitated by the fact that for them, as for all other students, tuition is free, they have a legal right to leave from work for study and there is a range of discretionary grants and loans. That many have responded is shown by the fact that in 1978 60% of all students were over 25. The figures for new students shown in Table 9.1 demonstrate that mature students are unevenly distributed between study lines. Within the mature student intake 48% were under 30, 42% between 30 and 39 and 10% aged 40 or over.

| | Percentages | | |
| --- | --- | --- | --- |
| | under 20 | 20 – 24 | over 24 |
| Technology | 43.1 | 42.2 | 14.5 |
| Administration | 31.3 | 37.3 | 31.5 |
| Care | 15.9 | 29.7 | 54.4 |
| Teaching | 14.7 | 28.6 | 56.6 |
| Culture | 31.1 | 35.5 | 33.3 |
| All lines | 31.9 | 37.2 | 30.8 |

**Table 9.1**
Mature Student Distribution by Field of Study: Autumn term intake 1979.[14]

Other interesting consequences of higher education reform have emerged. The more selective the entry to a field of study, for example the socio-medical and teacher training ones, the more necessary it has appeared to be to have work experience to be accepted, hence a better chance for adults. Each of the courses which make up a degree is given a points value according to its length and there is a strong tendency to enrol for single courses and particularly the shorter ones, rather than for a full degree programme. Of course students may come back later, in the recurrent education mode. In 1978 72% of all students were not enrolled for a full programme. At the same time nearly a third of students were part-timers, another significant rise. With all the reforms the percentage of students failing to complete the course or programme for which they have enrolled remains high. There is no evidence to link any of these phenomena with the increased proportion of adult students, however. Indeed there is evidence to suggest that drop-out is not unconnected with the persistence of the traditional 'take-it-or-leave-it' attitude to teaching.[15]

# Conclusion

It would be premature to draw conclusions yet from the practice of continuing education in the higher education systems of France, Federal Germany and Sweden. In each case it is based on fairly recent measures, which in France and Sweden have been repeatedly amended since they were first enacted. Either experience has shown that legislators did not get it right in the first place, or changing external conditions have required amendments to be made. It is still unclear what the long-term effects will be.[16] Nevertheless, some observations may be offered.

For the countries we have studied, committing universities to continuing education has been a radical departure from tradition. It has occurred within a wider reform of function, structure and governance, which, in each country, has brought universities together with other institutions into a single system of higher education. It may be of some significance for comparative purposes that United Kingdom universities have long been engaged in extra-mural work, albeit of a limited kind, that they have not been subject to radical reform of their organization and have remained in a distinct sector from the rest of higher education.

In France, Federal Germany and Sweden the obligation to undertake continuing education is laid down by law, but only in the last country is the enforcement of the law inherent in the text. In the other two the obligation is in effect moral, and institutions are encouraged rather than compelled to comply, although the power of compulsion is there should government wish to use it. The encouragement is, however, real and is backed by financial support. One may ask what difference it makes in the United Kingdom that the State does not have a similar legal right of compulsion. How different in nature and effect are government encouragements to continuing education under responsible body regulations or Pickup? It is true that continuing education activities take place widely in United Kingdom universities without legal obligation. Was legislation a necessary spur in the other three countries?

In Swedish higher education continuing education now occupies a central position and is a major function of all teaching departments. In France and Federal Germany it still occupies a marginal place. Continuing education services may come directly under the vice-chancellor or the central administration, but they are largely administrative and promotional agencies. The academic significance of their staff lies in their expertise in adult learning and teaching. So far, however, this field has had little recognition in higher education, even in Sweden. The fact that the academic departments are responsible for teaching and planning the content of courses might suggest closer involvement of the whole institution in continuing education. This could be so in the Federal Republic, where internal staff do most of the teaching, in some cases as part of their normal workload, but in French universities the fact that it is mostly done by staff hired from outside emphasizes its marginality.[17] None of these countries has chosen to recruit adult education subject tutors on the British model.

Reference has been made here to a wide range of kinds and levels of activities open to adults. The reform of higher education in France, Federal Germany and Sweden has had as one of its objectives the development of more vocationally oriented programmes. Not surprisingly there is a similar emphasis on continuing education. What is more surprising is the large amount of general interest provision. The main emphasis seems to be placed on four broad categories of activity: courses leading to degrees or diplomas; post-experience courses at graduate level not sanctioned by a formal award; other non-award bearing courses aimed at adults having higher education entrance qualifications or their equivalent; non-award bearing courses for a general public and specifying no educational level.

To varying extents France, Federal Germany and Sweden have widened access to standard undergraduate courses for adults who are without the appropriate school qualifications. Federal Germany, notably through the Distance University, and France, through face-to-face courses in conventional institutions, are providing award-bearing courses specifically aimed at adults.

Outside interests (employers, organized labour and other groups) are engaged in policy-making in different degrees. In Sweden they have a voice in the whole higher education system through their legal representation on regional and study line boards. In France and Federal Germany there appears to be uncertainty about the role they should play, in so far as there are wide divergences between institutions in those countries. In France, of course, they play a major role as direct clients of SUFCO, but in neither Federal Germany nor Sweden are they placed in that commanding position.

In each of the countries examined legal measures have been taken to facilitate the participation of adults in continuing education. These apply to continuing education in higher education. All three have enacted a legal right of employees to leave from work for education. The nature of this right is different in each one and it is not clear yet what influence it has had in each country. In Federal Germany it is a right to paid leave, in France the right to paid leave is hedged about with conditions, in Sweden leave and payments in lieu of earnings are not legally linked but there is an extensive provision of grants. In both France and Sweden a payroll tax on employers is intended to encourage them to provide or pay for continuing education, in higher education as in other sectors. There are special support measures for the unemployed and for other categories with special needs.

In each of the countries examined there is still not unanimous acceptance within higher education that it should engage in continuing education, nor, if it has to be done, is there general agreement about the form it should take. In each country there are signs that the weight of academic tradition is working against the realization of government plans. There are doubts too among the traditional providers of adult education, among employers and organized labour about higher education's ability to provide what is needed. Nevertheless, although progress may be slowed, there is no indication that it can be halted. Continuing education in higher education is here to stay.

There are still, however, uncertainties about the kind of provision that should be made, how it should be organized, whether it can fit into existing systems of higher education, or whether a radical reform is required, as in Sweden, and what should be the nature of this reform. The situation is complicated by the fact that higher education is under many other pressures. Many strong opinions have been expressed, but they are too often based on value judgements rather than reliable evidence. It is a field in which research is badly needed and since, as is shown here, many of the questions which need to be answered are not specific to any one country, there is a strong case for undertaking international comparative studies.

# References

1 Titmus, Colin (1976) Social pressures on Western European universities in the field of adult education *International Congress of University Adult Education Journal* XV (3) November

2 Loi d'Orientation de l'Enseignement Supérieur, 12 November, 1968

3 Loi du 16 juillet 1971 portant organisation de la formation professionnelle continue dans le cadre de l'éducation permanente

4 Circulaire du 72-187 du 26 avril 1972, Modalités d'application de la loi no. 71-575 du 16 juillet 1971 portant organisation de la formation continue...

5 *Le Guide de la Formation Continue dans les Universités Francaises* (1980) Conférence des Présidents d'Université/centre INFFO, Paris

6 Knoll, Joachim (1981) *Adult Education in the Federal Republic of Germany* Vancouver: University of British Columbia
   *Zentrale Einrichtungen/Kontaktstellen für Weiterbildung an Hochschulen* (1983) Beiträge No.16, Arbeitskreis Universitäre Erwachsenenbildung, Hanover

7 Hochschulrahmengesetz, 1976

8 Knoll *op. cit.*

9 Hochschule und Weiterbildung, 1/1983, Arbeitskreis Universitäre Erwachsenenbildung

10 *op. cit.* 6 above

11 *ibid.*

12 Hochschule und Weiterbildung, 1/1983 *op. cit.*

13 U68 Summary Utbildningsdepartment (1973) p. 8

14 Source UHÄ (1979) Numbers from Central Admissions, Autumn Term, 1979

15 For data quoted in the section on Swedish higher education I have drawn heavily on Boucher, Leon (1982) *Tradition and Change in Swedish Education* Oxford: Pergamon

16 Since this article was written I have received data to suggest that, as a result of deliberate government action, the proportion of students under 25 years of age in higher education in Sweden, has increased, at the expense, of course, of mature students. A new higher education law in France, which will come into force in 1986, will extend access to award-bearing courses for adults.

17 Freynet, P. (1982) *Un Service de Formation Continue et son Environnement* Thesis for the Doctorat du 3e cycle en Sciences de l'Education, University of Caen

# 10

# Jam Today?
# The UGC and NAB Reports

*Pat Fleetwood-Walker and Peter Toyne*

'The time has come' the Walrus said,
To talk of many things:
Of shoes – and ships – and sealing wax –
Of cabbages – and kings –
And why the sea is boiling hot –
And whether pigs have wings,
(Lewis Carroll *Through the Looking Glass* Ch. 4)

A friendly outsider, looking at what has been going on in higher education in Britain over the last few years, might well come to the conclusion that a similar edict to consider a wide range of disparate issues had been issued to everyone in the system by some kind of latter-day Carroll-like Walrus! For indeed, we *have* talked of many things: ranging from cuts, funds and FTE's to access, research, tenure, teaching and learning methods, academic organization, balance of curriculum, methods of validation and many other topics affecting the way in which the system operates and the way in which it might be developed. If, however, we were to look for a single edict-issuing Walrus which has triggered this wide-ranging debate and analysis we would be in difficulty since there have been several bodies instrumental in focusing our attention on specific issues. Nevertheless, foremost among those bodies must be the UGC and NAB which have both initiated major reviews of their respective sectors in recent years and to that extent may perhaps be regarded as a pair of Walrus-like edict-issuers, having substantial and fundamental influence in and on the present binary system.

## Terms of Reference of the UGC and NAB Groups

Both the UGC and NAB have, of course, been conducting a general and comprehensive review of their respective sectors but it is perhaps not without significance that they both decided, early on in those reviews, that the time had come to take a hard look at the role of continuing education within the higher education system. Both bodies established separate working groups (with cross-membership of the respective chairmen) for this specific purpose – the UGC in late 1982 and NAB early in 1983. Their terms of reference were broadly similar: the NAB group was asked

> to consider and advise on the appropriate role and extent of continuing education provision in the local authority sector and the policies and practices by which this provision might be fostered;

while the UGC group was given the remit to consider

a   the development of continuing education of all kinds in the universities;
b   the role of the UGC in these developments;
c   the financial arrangements including student support.

## First Impressions

Both working groups presented their reports in 1984 and perhaps the most striking thing about them is their extraordinary similarity. It might, after all, have been thought that the difference between the two sectors in terms of their courses, aspirations, historical backgrounds, ways of working, academic emphases and funding would have led to largely differing conclusions but, in fact, what emerges is a remarkable consistency between the two. And not only are the detailed conclusions and recommendations broadly similar, but both reports identify the need for a truly transbinary initiative if continuing education is to be developed actively in the years ahead. Above all, the common conclusion is that continuing education must be given a far greater priority not just in the universities, polytechnics, colleges and institutes of higher education but centrally within the educational establishment (DES, UGC, NAB and validating bodies) and in the world of industry, commerce and the professions. In order to achieve that higher priority, both working groups recognize that a fundamental change of attitude on the part of all concerned would be necessary and, in that sense, the reports are nothing less than revolutionary.

## Objectives behind the Reports

The pulse had clearly been quickening for some time, with more and more interest being shown in developing continuing education in principle, just as the pressure of potentially declining numbers of (traditional) students in higher education was beginning to make the institutions themselves more than willing to consider implementing the principle, which may otherwise have been destined to remain an interesting pipedream. Given this situation the UGC and NAB had no real alternative but to consider what should be done. Perhaps for this reason, as we have seen already, the remit given to the NAB working group was not just one of looking at what was happening but actually of finding ways in which the provision 'might be fostered'. To many, this was nothing short of remarkable, since at that time everything else that NAB was doing appeared to be the antithesis of fostering anything. The

UGC group for its part was asked to define what they saw to be the universities' 'distinctive role' in continuing education and to examine potential links with the public sector, in the hope of developing joint initiatives. Again, remarkable – because the universities were not exactly renowned for wanting to collaborate with the public sector.

# The Current State of Continuing Education

Both working groups began their analyses by assessing the extent of present provision and by reviewing the reasons why continuing education was becoming an increasing necessity before attempting to identify the barriers to access which prevented the realization of the potential contribution of continuing education to the higher education system. Perhaps it came as something of a surprise to both groups that the extent of present provision was as great as it turned out to be – and that is saying something, since both working groups consisted of members who have considerable experience of continuing education. In fact the NAB report contains a useful summary of the estimated provision in both sectors (this being possible because theirs was not completed until after the publication of the UGC report). Two rather different kinds of continuing education courses are revealed – those leading to recognized qualifications, and those which are commonly labelled short courses and do not normally lead to an award.

# The First Barrier – Inadequate Statistics

Both groups had very great difficulty in getting any reliable estimate of short course activities in their respective sectors because so many simply go unrecorded in any official statistical records (and often, indeed, in the institutions themselves). Indeed, so great was the difficulty that the NAB group observed that 'the inadequacy of the short course data makes a realistic estimate of numbers impossible', and went on to conclude that 'as far as the public sector is concerned the only way forward is the collection of reliable statistics' (NAB Report, para. 3.25). For this reason one of its earliest recommendations (No. 2 of 41) was that NAB should 'establish an annual published summary of all advanced short course provision which will provide details on students numbers and lengths of course by (NAB) programme area.' The weary and fainthearted may be forgiven for thinking that such a recommendation was an inevitable and predictable product of a NAB working group, but the concern was very real that, without adequate evidence of the scale of these activities, it would be impossible to make adequate provision for them within the NAB planning exercise. The UGC working group faced similar problems with regard to short courses and concluded that 'the Universities' Statistical Record (USR) may underestimate the real level of activity' in courses run by academic departments, although the statistics from extra-mural departments were known to be much more precise. The matching recommendation for the UGC was: 'We recommend that universities and the USR should obtain more complete statistical information in respect of short courses.'

## Facts and Figures

Quantitative evidence about the scale of award-bearing courses which might be regarded as an essential part of continuing education provision was, in comparison, easier to unearth – though the usual difficulties of definition and interpretation were at once apparent. It was estimated that in 1982-83 there were some 31,520 'mature' entrants to full-time and sandwich first-degree and diploma courses in public sector institutions and 8,850 full-time mature students in the university sector, making a total of some 40,000 mature entrants. In addition there were approximately 11,000 mature entrants to full-time postgraduate courses of which about 75% were, not surprisingly perhaps, in the universities. Estimation of total part-time mature entrants on award-bearing courses was found to be more difficult because the UGC classes all part-time students as mature, while the evidence is that in the public sector less than 75% of them are thus categorized. At the undergraduate level this is less significant, as the NAB report points out, since 'the universities' total of 4,781 is dwarfed by the 10,000 degree and 60,000 non-degree entrants in the public sector.' However, at postgraduate level it *is* more significant, since the UGC records some 25,000 mature part-time students while the public sector records only about 5,500. In addition, of course, the Open University has some 20,000 to 25,000 entrants each year, and if these were to be included in the statistics, it would appear that there are in excess of 90,000 'mature' entrants to part-time degree or non-degree courses per annum in the UK. In other words, the scale of continuing education, estimated in both reports, is by no means insignificant – rather, it is far more substantial than many had perhaps been led (or prepared) to believe.

## Arguing the Case

Having demonstrated the extent of present provision, both groups had something to say about why continuing education was needed. This may well seem rather odd to the outsider: after all, if continuing education is on as extensive a scale as it appears to be, it hardly seems necessary to say why it is needed. Perhaps it is merely a sign of the times in which we live that even groups as prestigious as those of NAB and the UGC feel they have to justify every single activity, however well-rooted and established it may be; but equally, of course, since both groups were clearly charged with considering how to extend this particular activity (already on a larger scale than they had perhaps anticipated), they obviously felt that some justification for it would be called for. And so, the NAB report contains a whole (though relatively short) chapter on 'The Need for Continuing Education' the conclusion of which is that continuing education has three functions to perform: viz – to contribute to the nation's economic needs ('the future need of the economy for highly qualified manpower which increasingly cannot be met by an 18-year-old age group whose population is declining' – para. 4); to contribute to the nation's social needs ('the increasing incidence of unemployment, early retirement and shorter working hours will mean that continuing education has an important function in helping people to enjoy and make greater use of their leisure' – para. 4.13); and to contribute to the needs of individuals for personal enjoyment, satisfaction and development. The report concludes rather loftily and optimistically, that 'there is no dilemma between meeting the needs of the economy,...the needs of society...and the aspirations of individuals....Rather these triple objectives must be seen as mutually reinforcing elements of a coherent strategy of increased support for continuing education.' Fine words indeed: we may all say 'Amen' to that. There then follows a splendid 'cap-in-hand' plaintive cry – the real rub – for money to be put where the rhetoric ends: 'The benefits which will flow from an investment in continuing education should not be sacrificed for the comparatively small sums of expenditure which will bring them about.' 'Amen', again!

The UGC group started from a different position, in that the university sector had a tradition of protecting liberal adult education through the separate funding of extra-mural departments. There was no intention of dismissing 'the importance of social, cultural and other factors' in deciding that the 'case for development of continuing education is largely founded on consideration of employment and economic prosperity'...but no one could deny that an alarm bell sounded when the group reflected on 'the rapid pace of technological, scientific and social change' coupled with the low rate of turnover of people in employment (and the regular updating of knowledge which both of these trends call for [UGC Report, paras. 6-9]). They were mindful of the Hodgkinson dictum of 1982, '90 per cent of the workforce in 1990 is already at work today,' with all that that means so far as the need to update and retrain the existing manpower to meet skills shortages is concerned. This kind of updating is already insufficient to keep employees abreast of new developments and we have a major shortfall in skilled manpower in those very areas (information technology, electronics) which are crucial to our economic survival (Butcher 1984; NEDC 1984). In arguing the case as it did, the UGC had already begun to redefine its priorities in favour of science and technology.

## Further Barriers to Expansion

After thus setting the scene upon which the real drama is to be enacted, both groups go on to look at the so-called 'barriers' to the development of continuing education (the lack of reliable data has already been referred to). Once more, the cynics may well have thought that an extended perambulation through the thickets of academia would be unavoidable and that the two groups would scarcely have the nerve to spell out what one would assume to be the real barrier – ie cash. But cynics were to be confounded because neither group ducked the issue. It is true that their reviews are comprehensive and touch on very many perceived barriers (some of which may even appear to be trendily hard-hitting of academics themselves) but the issue of finance tends to appear as a significant leitmotif throughout the discourse. There is, even so, another leitmotif, one which is even more dominant than the 'finance' theme – and this is about 'attitude changes'. It is spelt out more explicitly by the NAB group, but is still all-pervasively evident throughout the UGC report too; and what it all adds up to is that there will be no significant development of continuing education unless attitudes to it change markedly. In particular, the cry appears to go up to institutions and individual academics that they should re-think their attitude to continuing education so that this kind of work does not simply exist as a useful (and extensive) 'add-on' to more traditional academic pursuits but becomes at least an equal partner in the academic pecking order of priorities.

The barriers are helpfully classified into three categories by the NAB group and whilst the UGC group may not have been quite so explicit or so keen to categorize (incidentally categorization is something which tends to happen a great deal in the NAB report) their findings are essentially the same. The three categories are 'providers, students and employers' (NAB Report, para. 5), and the list of identified barriers really does represent a fair indictment of them all, even though it is acknowledged that 'of course, these difficulties do not apply to all institutions or students or employers' (para. 5.3). 'Not half,' must come the reply, 'but there must be a very large number to whom they *do* apply, otherwise it would not have been worthwhile mentioning it.' Within the university sector one of the crucial barriers to increasing continuing education lies in the low status of the activity, compared particularly with research. Not only is career advancement almost exclusively dependent upon research but the 1981 cuts have, if anything, exacerbated the situation. What we must make sure of now is that all universities take up this new emphasis, so that we achieve an attitude change throughout the system.

## Barriers affecting the Providers

If we look at the two reports together, the list of barriers begins with 'providers' (which really means 'institutions') and nine major barriers are identified. Reading this list, the academic may well feel very uncomfortable: it is painfully like going to the doctor to be told in words of one syllable what you had secretly feared all along. First, we are told that we provide inadequate information and guidance facilities for mature students, 'that we have an insufficiently market-oriented approach to post-experience vocational education', and that our courses 'are not suited to meet continuing education objectives in terms of mode of attendance, context, length, level and delivery.' 'Good Heavens,' we may well wonder, 'is there anything else left, is there nothing we have got right?' The answer comes quickly – it is direct and worrying and takes the form: 'Yes, there is much more to come and, no, there is not much you have got right.' And so, we are next told that we exhibit 'lack of flexibility over entry requirements,' that we have 'negative staff attitudes and inappropriate staff skills' and that we provide 'inadequate facilities for mature student needs.' After this full-frontal attack on our academic prowess and stance, we might well feel a sense of relief – of being 'let off the hook' – at the final three indictments, of the providers, since they appear to be getting one in at our masters (both outside and inside our institutions). The charge is read that the next barriers are 'government policy to move to full cost fees for post-experience vocational education', the 'low weighting given to part-time provision in resource allocation and grading of work' and a 'lack of recognition and other incentives for staff who promote continuing education'. At the end of the charge sheet, we are tempted to marvel that we have *already* delivered such an extensive provision of continuing education programmes, given the seriousness and extent of the accusations made. But that simply has to be put down to academic escapism, because we all know the essential if exaggerated truth of what has been said, and we all know that we do need to face reality. The more worrying thing, however, is that many of our colleagues may seek refuge from the storm by pointing to the last three identified barriers as the main obstacles to development and, in so doing, may not sufficiently take up the real academic challenge of the working groups, which seem to us to be to do with inculcating a real change of individual and institutional attitude to mature students and their need.

## Barriers affecting Students

In comparison, the eight barriers or difficulties which the groups claim confront students may at first sight appear to be less fundamentally challenging of the status quo. In fact they are every bit as serious as those affecting the providers – and, indeed, two of them are more a reflection of the providers' attitudes than of the students' own making. Thus, 'inadequate information and guidance' is merely a repetition of the barrier earlier ascribed to the providers, while 'inadequate credit transfer and work recognition arrangements' is simply a specific aspect of the providers' 'lack of flexibility over entry requirements'. (This latter point, interestingly, is taken up at some length in both reports and results in quite specific recommendations about the development of credit accumulation and transfer systems [including the granting of credit for work experience] across the binary line – revolutionary stuff indeed!) All the other six identified barriers are, however, no more than a list of the already well-known difficulties facing mature students – lack of confidence, suitable educational qualifications and general educational preparedness, lack of leisure and study time, geographical and travel problems in getting to the providing institution, high fees and other costs of study, non-existent or inadequate student maintenance grants and (a marvellously bland, catch-all expression) 'family responsibilities'. While recognizing the same barriers, the UGC group expressed particular concern about 'present policies on library access for short course students' and recommended that they be examined 'with a view to removing as many restrictions as possible' (UGC Report, para. 46).

## Barriers affecting Employers

The employers, the third group to be identified, are given quite a grilling too – though it does seem as if the academics (the providers) come in for most of the stick. Four problems, however, are laid firmly at the feet of the employers: first, it is said that they display a 'reluctance or inability to pay high costs for retraining or updating' their workforce, and it is alleged that they are similarly reluctant or unable 'to provide staff with leave of absence or paid leave for approved educational purposes'; there then follows what is in reality the most worrying charge, that they have 'inadequate longer term awareness of their own needs for updating and retraining'. That statement has to be read several times over before the jargon begins to crack and its true message appears – and when it does it is nothing short of alarming, for it really means that employers have no idea what they want or need. In the circumstances the academics might perhaps be forgiven their sins of academic omission and commission in attempting to provide anything at all. The last 'employer' barrier is seen to be 'inadequate longer term support for employees and educational institutions' and, again, when stripped of its committee-speak, the conclusion is every bit as alarming as the previous observation. Taken together, these four barriers attributable to the employers are particularly disturbing, since collectively they strike at the very heart of the problem and simply tell us that unless something is done very soon to rectify the situation all the best efforts of the providers to put their house in order will be to little real avail, since the employers will neither know what they want nor have the means of delivering the students. So much for *fostering* continuing education. Of course, many employers have rushed in to deny the charges when they are writ large in black and white, but neither the UGC nor the NAB group dreamed them up – they both went to considerable lengths to consult widely with employers and to identify their perceived needs and difficulties and the four observations merely stem from those consultations.

## Recommendations for overcoming the Barriers

Once the barriers to the development of continuing education had been identified, the two groups were in a position to suggest how they might be overcome. Again, it is the remarkable similarity between the two groups' recommendations which is noteworthy and encouraging – if, as we have said earlier, it is also somewhat surprising. In summing up, the UGC group finally made twenty-three recommendations, while the NAB group made forty-one, and they can be grouped broadly into four categories according to their subject.

1   Eleven of the forty-one recommendations made by NAB and sixteen of the twenty-three by the UGC were directly concerned with *changing institutional attitudes and procedures, content and delivery* (NAB 15-25 and UGC a, c, h-t).
2   *Finance and methods of student support* were covered by NAB 26-27 and UGC d-f and w.
3   Recommendations about the *establishment of new national committees* – perhaps the most important group since they covered overseeing and developing continuing education in the future – were NAB 38-41 and UGC b.
4   Three recommendations (NAB 1-3 and UGC v) were concerned with arrangements for *monitoring, surveying and publishing coordinated information on continuing education*. It is important to stress that in the view of the NAB working group nearly a half of these recommendations related to changes in the attitude and behaviour of institutions, a point

which was made by a single cover-all statement by the UGC in recommendation h: 'that universities should take steps to encourage staff to regard continuing education as an integral part of their role.'

# Recommendations to Whom?

## *To Employers*

A rather more revealing way of categorizing the recommendations of the two reports is, however, afforded by grouping them according to whom they were addressed. Three main target groups can be identified:- the Government (or DES), the parent body (NAB/UGC), and the institutions themselves. The striking and obvious observation is, however, that employers appear to have been largely ignored in the actual recommendations. The NAB group made only one relevant recommendation (the very last one, 41), and, on the face of it, it is very mild indeed in comparison to most others: 'We recommend *companies* to seek longer term relationships with their local institutions in considering their updating needs and how they might be met.' Lurking behind this recommendation, however, is a paragraph of rather finer exhortation: 'The efforts of polytechnics and colleges to respond positively to the proposals in this report will require a matching response from employers to articulate their needs more clearly, to be willing to engage in dialogue with local institutions and in a greater degree of joint planning, and to make greater financial and other commitments which a successful programme will require' (NAB Report, para. 11) Even so, the employers appear to have been put off-stage – which is unfortunate in view of the centrally important role they play in creating student demand and the vehement criticism levelled at them in the main report. The UGC report, despite extensive discussions with them, is strangely silent with regard to employers, making no specific recommendations that relate chiefly to them.

## *To the Government*

The recommendations made to government were, of course, mainly directed through the DES – though some of those in the NAB report were primarily intended for the local education authorities. In all, some fourteen recommendations were made to the DES and four to the LEAs by the NAB group, and one directly to government by the UGC group. They are, in the main, concerned with increasing financial provision, but also deal with the development of guidance services, access to courses and credit accumulation and transfer systems (NAB Recommendations 9, 16 and 40). The latter is, in many ways, again rather remarkable since it calls for a transbinary initiative to be made on credit transfer and it is matched by a similar call from the UGC group. Who would have imagined, only a few years ago, that this particular subject would be taken up with such apparent enthusiasm? It is, however, with financial easement that most of the recommendations to the DES are concerned. The most important obviously relate to the level of funding which is needed in order to promote continuing education. The NAB group asks for 'a 25% increase in resourcing for part-time provision to be achieved over the next 3 years,' and goes on to request 'as a first instalment, an improvement in resourcing of 10% amounting to £15m agreed for 1985-86' (Recommendation 28). In addition it recommends that '£5m be added to the AFE pool from 1985-86 onwards for the purposes of pump priming PEVE' (Recommendation 36). The thorny problem of student grants was also addressed and three particularly important NAB recommendations are directed at this difficult area: that the DES should 'agree to grants being made available for any part of a designated course studied full-time' (Recommendation 23), 'undertake as a matter of urgency a review of the financial support arrangements for mature students on full time courses with a view to providing a larger measure of support and adjusting arrangements which cause particular hardship' (Recommendation 26), and give 'serious consideration...to the possibility of providing tax relief for PEVE students' (Recommendation 35). The equally difficult subject of the purpose and effects of fees was covered by the recommendation that the DES should 'undertake a comprehensive review of the purpose and effects of fees in higher education, and that in the meantime the fees for part-time students across all sectors should be set at a lower level' (Recommendation 30). Finally, the institutional funding arrangements for part-time students in the public sector came in for scrutiny, and the NAB group concluded that not only should the full-time equivalent weightings for part-time students be revised (upwards) but that institutions should 'review their internal resource allocation policies to ensure that they offer adequate encouragement to the development of part-time work' (Recommendation 29). (In other words, are enough internal financial carrots being offered to departments?) The UGC group's financial recommendations are along the same lines, if rather less explicit in some respects, but they additionally recommend increased resourcing of post-experience vocational education courses, because 'universities should be encouraged to increase their provision. Fees for such courses should cover directly attributable costs but the UGC should seek additional funds from Government in order to enable it to make an allocation in recurrent grant of approximately £500 per FTE PEVE student' (Recommendation c). The additional monies needed are estimated at £2.5m. The UGC group, particularly troubled by the low grant available for part-time students, asked that 'in order to encourage universities to provide more part-time degree and diploma opportunities, the UGC should provide grant commensurate with that given for full-time students (Recommendation d). In so doing it was recognized that this increase would have to come out of existing resources (ie with a commensurate decrease in the pool of money available for full-time students). On the face of it, Recommendation f covers policies regarding 'responsible body' status (extra-mural departments), but there is a financial implication. A number of universities, particularly the quarter or so denied extra-mural departments, could see no reason why the remit to provide liberal adult education should not be shared by all.

## *To NAB and the UGC*

The second broad set of recommendations was directed to the 'parent bodies' as we have labelled them, that is to NAB and the UGC themselves. Again, the NAB report is rather more explicit than its counterpart but the terms are much the same. In the case of NAB, the recommendations include those relating to finance and two other very important ones which show just how determined the group were to see continuing education flourish. Many of the recommendations to the DES were also recommendations to NAB itself. The first was that NAB should establish a standing group of its Board with immediate responsibility for conveying forward work on the outstanding issues identified in the report – thus ensuring the continuation of the momentum generated so far – but the second was a very interesting one indeed because it tackled head on a subject which, to some, is seen as taboo – viz, the promotion of the humanities. The recommendation is simply put: 'We further recommend NAB to agree to institutions' proposals to increase numbers in the humanities area where this is for part-time provision' (Recommendation 18). But what a marvellous minefield that is! Here is a recommendation to NAB from one of its own working groups, asking for explicit provision of increased numbers in an area which continues to be regarded with the greatest suspicion and which is clearly one of the least-favoured academic sons. Someone, somewhere, on reading this must at least have thought, in Red Queen-like fashion, 'Off with their heads!' In contrast, the UGC group emphasized the expansion of post-experience vocational education courses, but this arose from a rather sharp shock received by reflection on the statistics, which show that 'PEVE courses' remain 'concentrated in traditional areas such as medicine and education and the provision in engineering, science and other vocational courses is disappointingly low' (para. 85). Though it must be noted that, in the words of the chairman, 'Our report encourages developments in the field of post-experience vocational educational needs of adults, for it envisages continuing education as a fully integrated function in the mainstream of university life encompassing liberal extra-mural provision and much more besides' (Chairman's Introduction).

## To the Institutions

As we have said before, the majority of recommendations were to the institutions themselves and they covered such related matters as:

- improved *attitudes* towards the whole activity – encouragement by institutions and acceptance on the part of staff;
- *support* from institutions – through new organizations (UGC), new academic boards and an influential person to direct (NAB);
- *incentives* to individuals through promotion procedures and to departments by sharing in the revenues;
- increase in *PEVE courses*;
- more attention to teaching methods for adults;
- development of *modular part-time courses* and timetables adapted to the needs of mature students;
- development of *credit transfer systems* and acceptance of *experiential learning*;
- more effort in *external liaison*, fostering *demand* and *marketing*;

- development of a consistent *policy on fees*;
- more flexible and speedy *response* from institutions – distance learning and outreach courses run in industry;
- more *help for students* – improved course information, counselling services, access courses (NAB) and improved library services for students on short courses;
- recognition of the *needs* of the unemployed and women returning to study;
- more *research* into continuing education.

## Conclusions

It can thus be seen that the two reports were both hard-hitting and wide-ranging. They were also remarkably optimistic and consistently positive in their recommendations, though it seems to us that they did tend to place rather too much emphasis and onus on the institutions and the 'educational' side of the house to get things moving. It would not have gone amiss if rather more stress had been placed on the ways in which employers can be brought into this important area of academic development – indeed, it could be argued that it is something of a nonsense to contemplate the kind of extensive development envisaged in both reports without a much greater involvement of employers than appears to be suggested in either of them. In fact, both groups did recognize this need, and that, undoubtedly, was the point in making the observations they did. But, with hindsight, simply looking at the balance of recommendations, it might have been better to have examined in more detail than was possible what form that role might take.

The big question now remains: will any of these laudable recommendations bear any fruit? The prognostications look hopeful. Within a matter of weeks of the publication of the second report (NAB) the DES announced its intention of acting on the recommendation to set up a national standing committee on continuing education across the binary line. Such breathtaking alacrity has scarcely been seen before and we can but hope that it may act as a spur at the institutional level to get on with the job of developing continuing education in an active and positive manner. Again, the first-fruits appear to be coming forth: units, professors and deans of continuing education have been established in several institutions and some are beginning to review their attitudes, their facilities and their teaching and learning methods accordingly. Another sign of subsequent progress is the acceptance of 'continuing education' by the UGC Main Committee as a 'major responsibility of the universities along with their responsibilities for teaching full-time students and for research' (UGC 1984). This decision represents a very substantial change in attitudes, achieved only after considerable discussion, and an outsider could be forgiven for not realizing what a change of heart this rather mild statement represents. It will take time, as both reports pointed out, to bring about so fundamental a change in attitudes and course provision, but the authors are of the firm view that development must start at the grass roots – in the attitudes and commitment of individual members of staff and of institutions. It will, as again both reports indicated, also require some additional finance, and we all know very well that that is probably a much more difficult thing to secure, especially in times of shrinking resources for higher education. The rhetoric and the analyses are now complete: it is now a question of getting some action and of translating heartfelt words into effective deeds. We fear that it would be all too easy for those same edict-issuing Walruses to reply to our pleas for the resources with which to deliver the hoped for development by using the words of Lewis Carroll's Walrus:

'I weep for you' the Walrus said:
'I deeply sympathise'...

But, as the White Queen would say:
'The rule is, jam to-morrow and jam yesterday –
but never jam to-day.'

Even so, we hope that our concerted efforts will increasingly build on the positive recommendations of the UGC and NAB Reports and that, as Alice said 'It *must* come sometimes to "jam to-day".'

# Further Reading

ACACE (1982) *Continuing Education: From Policies to Practice*

Butcher, J. (1984) *The Human Factor: the Supply Side Problem* First Report, IT Skills Shortages Committee

CVCP and UCAE (1980) *The Universities and Continuing Education*

DES (1980) *Continuing Education: Post-experience Vocational Provision for those in Employment* A paper for discussion

Hodgkinson, H. L. (1982) *Guess Who's Coming to College*, NIICU Research Report. Washington DC: National Institute of Independent Colleges and Universities

Manpower Services Commission (1983) *Adult Training Strategy*

National Advisory Body (1984) *Report of the Continuing Education Group*

NEDC (1984) *Crisis Facing UK Information Technology*

Tight, M. (1982) *Part-Time Degree Study in the United Kingdom* ACACE

University Grants Committee (1984) *Report of the Continuing Education Working Party*

University Grants Committee (1984) *A Strategy for Higher Education into the 1990's* London: HMSO

# The Authors

TYRRELL BURGESS is Reader in the Philosophy of Social Institutions and Dean of Continuing Education at North East London Polytechnic. His previous posts at the polytechnic were Director of the Centre for Institutional Studies and Head of the School for Independent Study. His books include *Education After School* (1977) and studies (with John Pratt) of the colleges of advanced technology (1970) and the polytechnics (1974) and (with Michael Locke and John Pratt) of the colleges of higher education (forthcoming). He is a member of the Education for Capability Committee of the Royal Society of Arts.

KITTY CHISHOLM attended schools in Washington DC and Athens, Greece and graduated in classics at Girton College in 1969. She is Administrative Assistant with the Open University in the SATUP (Scientific and Technological Updating Programme) Sector of Continuing Education. She has been with the Open University as student, tutor, research assistant and course co-ordinator since 1972, responsible for administration of the liaison between the Open University and the Manpower Services Commission since 1983. She is an enthusiastic amateur of IT, interested in the pre-Platonic development of logic.

PATRICIA FLEETWOOD-WALKER is an educationalist with research interests in the design and evaluation of courses and information-gathering skills among professionals: doctors and managers. Originally a biologist, she held a series of posts at Birmingham and Aston Universities, where she worked as a consultant on matters related to teaching and learning across the full range of university disciplines. Currently Director of Extension Education, she has a keen interest in continuing professional development and has been a member of the UGC Working Party on Continuing Education and its successor – the Joint UGC/NAB Continuing Education Standing Committee.

KEITH PERCY has degrees in history, sociology and adult education from the Universities of Cambridge, London and Nottingham. He is currently Organizing Tutor for Extra-Mural Studies and Lecturer in Educational Research in the University of Lancaster. He has directed a number of research projects into provision of, and participation in, education and training for adults and includes among his current research interests education of older adults, independent learning and learning in non-formal organization.

MICHAEL RICHARDSON is Pro Vice-Chancellor (Continuing Education) at the Open University. He studied at Cambridge and Nottingham Universities. Since joining the Open University he has worked as Deputy Regional Director (North), Regional Director (North West), and Director of the Centre for Continuing Education. Prior to that he was Warden and Principal of Alfreton Hall Adult Education Centre. His research interests are in the structure and policy of continuing education and in the implication of 'non-work' on education for adults. He has chaired and authored for Open University courses on the training of Adult Education, and jointly with Neil Costello edited *Continuing Education for the Post Industrial Society* (1982).

GORDON RODERICK, a graduate and a PhD in physics, entered adult education as a science tutor after work in scientific research. He later moved into administration and adult teacher 'training', firstly at Liverpool University and subsequently at Sheffield University and at University College, Swansea. His research interests lie mainly in the history of education, in particular in scientific and technical education, but also in aspects of higher education and of general adult education. His publications include *The Emergence of a Scientific Society in England, 1800-1965*, *Education and Industry in Nineteenth Century England* and *Never Too Late to Learn*. Co-edited works include *Mature Students in Higher and Further Education in Sheffield*, *Universities for a Changing World*, *Where Did We Go Wrong? Industry, Education and Economy in Victorian Britain* and *The British Malaise. Industry, Education and Economy in Britain Today*.

R. A. SHEPHERD, a graduate of Cambridge University, joined the Ford Motor Company in 1950, where he is currently Manager, Education, Training and Personnel Services. He was a member of the 'Hayes' Committee on training for the management of human resources and of an EEC Working Party on the use of Social Aid Funds for vocational training. He has been a member of the Education and Training Committees of the Technical Education Council and the Business Education Council and of the Confederation of British Industry. He is a member of the BTEC Continuing Education Committee, acting Chairman of the Action Committee administering the National Engineering Scholarship Scheme, a Governor of North East London Polytechnic and Chairman of the Training of Trainers Advisory Group.

COLIN TITMUS is a graduate of London University who, after a number of years as a school teacher, joined the University of Glasgow Department of Adult and Continuing Education, where he was in charge of graduate studies in adult education. Since 1981 he has been Dean of Adult and Community Studies at the University of London Goldsmiths' College. A specialist in comparative adult education, he has lectured at universities in France, Federal Germany and Canada. He has been a consultant to

UNESCO, OECD and the Council of Europe. His publications include *Adult Education in France* and *Strategies for Adult Education*. He is chief editor of the *UNESCO Terminology of Adult Education* and editor of the Adult, Recurrent and Lifelong Education section of the *International Encyclopedia of Education*.

PETER TOYNE is Deputy Rector at the North East London Polytechnic. He was previously Deputy Director at West Sussex Institute of Higher Education and before that was Senior Lecturer in Geography and Sub-Dean of Social Studies at the University of Exeter. He has been closely involved in the development of credit transfer in higher education, having been Director of the DES Feasibility Study and author of the Toyne Report which led to the establishment of the ECCTIS pilot scheme which is now operating in South-West England. He served as a member of the NAB Continuing Education Group and he is at present Chairman of the Initial Training and Education Panel of the Council for the Education and Training of Youth and Community Workers and a member of the CNAA Combined Studies (Humanities) Board.

MAUREEN WOODHALL is currently Lecturer in Educational Administration at the University of London Institute of Education, where she was previously Senior Research Officer. She has carried out research in many areas of the economics of education, particularly the costs and finance of education, cost-benefit analysis, manpower forecasting and educational planning. She has been a consultant for OECD, UNESCO, the World Bank, the Open University and the Overseas Students Trust. She has published widely on the economics of education, including three books on student loans. Her more recent book, with George Psacharopoulos, is *Education for Development: Analysis of Investment Choices*.

# Index of References

# The Society for Research into Higher Education

*The Society for Research into Higher Education exists to encourage and co-ordinate research and development in all aspects of higher education. It thus draws to public attention both the need for research and development and the needs of the research community. Its income is derived from subscriptions, and from research or other specific grants. It is wholly independent. Its corporate members are universities, polytechnics, institutes of higher education, research institutions and professional and governmental bodies. Its individual members are teachers and researchers, administrators and students. Members are found in all parts of the world and the Society regards its international work as amongst its most important activities.*

*The Society discusses and comments on policy, organizes conferences and sponsors research. Under the imprint SRHE & NFER-NELSON it is a specialist publisher of research, having over 30 titles in print. It also publishes* Studies in Higher Education *(three times a year),* Higher Education Abstracts *(three times a year),* International Newsletter *(twice a year), a* Bulletin *(six times a year), and, jointly with the Committee for Research into Teacher Education (CRITE)* Evaluation Newsletter *(twice a year).*

*The Society's committees, study groups and local branches are run by members, with help from a small secretariat, and aim to provide a forum for discussion. Some of the groups, at present the Teacher Education Study Group and the Staff Development Group, have their own subscriptions and organization, as do some Regional Branches. The Governing Council, elected by members, comments on current issues and discusses policies with leading figures in politics and education. The Society organizes seminars on current research for officials of the DES and other ministries, and is in touch with bodies in Britain such as the CNAA, NAB, CVCP, UGC and the British Council; and with sister-bodies overseas. Its current research projects include one on the relationship between entry qualifications and degree results, directed by Prof. W.D. Furneaux (Brunel) and one on 'Questions of Quality' directed by Prof. G.C. Moodie (York).*

*The Society's annual conferences take up central themes, viz. 'Continuing Education' (1985, organized in collaboration with Goldsmiths' College, the Open University and the University of Surrey, with advice from the DES and the CBI), 'Standards and criteria in HE' (1986) 'Restructuring' (1987). Joint conferences are held, viz. on the DES 'Green Paper' (1985, with* The Times Higher Education Supplement) *and on 'Information Technology' (1986, with the Council for Educational Technology, the Computer Board and the Universities of Glasgow and Strathclyde) and on 'The Freshman Year' (1986, with the University of South Carolina and Newcastle Polytechnic). For some of the Society's conferences, special studies are commissioned in advance, as 'Precedings'.*

*Members receive free of charge the Society's* Abstracts, *annual conference proceedings (or 'Precedings'), and* Bulletin *and* International Newsletter, *and may buy SRHE & NFER-NELSON books at booksellers' discount. Corporate members receive the Society's journal* Studies in Higher Education *free, individuals at a heavy discount. They may also obtain* Evaluation Newsletter *and certain other journals at discount, including the NFER* Register of Educational Research.

*Further information may be obtained from the Society for Research into Higher Education, At the University, Guildford GU2 5XH, UK.*